Essential SQA Exam Practice

Higher Modern Studies

Practice Questions & Exam Papers

Questions & Papers

▶ Practise **extended questions** for every question type

▶ Complete **2 practice papers** that mirror the real SQA exams

Frank Cooney

HODDER GIBSON
AN HACHETTE UK COMPANY

The Publishers would like to thank the following for permission to reproduce copyright material.

Acknowledgements

pp. 15–16, practice question 19 and corresponding marking instructions taken from SQA 2018 Specimen Question Paper 2 © Scottish Qualifications Authority; *source A:* article is adapted from '"Jihadi Jack" Letts interview: Former Oxford schoolboy calls on British people to convert to Islam as he brands David Cameron an "evil creature"' by Shebab Khan, taken from *The Independent,* 30 January 2016 (2018 SQP page 7); *source B:* graph is adapted from 'Issues facing Britain — What do you see as the biggest issue facing the UK today?' © Ipsos MORI (2018 SQP page 7); *source C:* screenshot of Channel 4 News website — "Do we know why we're in Afghanistan" by Jon Snow, 28 July 2009 © Channel 4 TV (2018 SQP page 8); **p.49,** *source C,* used by kind permission of The Prescription Charges Coalition, www.prescriptionchargescoalition.org.uk; **p.59,** source A, The Electoral Commission; **p.60,** *source C,* graph is adapted from 'Trouble for the EU after Brexit?'© Ipsos MORI.

© Frank Cooney 2019

First published in 2019 by
Hodder Gibson, an imprint of Hodder Education
An Hachette UK Company
211 St Vincent Street
Glasgow, G2 5QY

Impression number	5	4	3	2	1
Year	2023	2022	2021	2020	2019

Illustrations by Aptara Inc.

Typeset in India by Aptara Inc.

Printed and bound by CPI Group (UK) Ltd, Croydon CR0 4YY

A catalogue record for this title is available from the British Library.

ISBN: 978 1 5104 7182 5

MIX
Paper from responsible sources
FSC™ C104740
www.fsc.org

SCOTLAND EXCEL

We are an approved supplier on the Scotland Excel framework.

Schools can find us on their procurement system as:

Hodder & Stoughton Limited t/a Hodder Gibson.

CONTENTS

INTRODUCTION

Higher Modern Studies

Welcome to your Essential Exam Practice for Higher Modern Studies. We hope that it will become an indispensable tool as you navigate through your revision for the Higher Modern Studies Exam Papers 1 and 2.

This book will show you how to unlock the specific types of exam questions that will appear in both papers, and equip you with the necessary knowledge, skills and experience to tackle both exam papers confidently.

The book contains two sections:

▶ Section 1 gives guidance on how to answer each of the seven question types that you can expect to encounter in the exams. Model student answers make clear the range of marks awarded for various sentences, sections, paragraphs and complete responses.

▶ Section 2 includes two full exam papers with complete marking instructions for you to attempt at home or in class. You may wish to time yourself to make sure that you can answer questions in the time allotted. This will improve your time management and help you avoid having to rush your questions, or even worse missing out some questions.

Here are some common-sense tips to prepare you for the exam.

Study skills – what you need to know to pass exams

So, you think you know how to revise and study effectively? Do you use the time wisely, or do you lose concentration and find excuses to do something else? The first step to improve your study skills involves the following points:

▶ Start revision in good time and do not leave it to the last moment.
▶ Make a revision timetable that balances time to study with time to relax.
▶ Make sure you have a copy of an up-to-date textbook (The *How to Pass Higher Modern Studies* textbook would be a great addition), along with your class notes, handouts and PowerPoints.
▶ Find a copy of the course outlines of the topics you will answer in your exam. The Course Assessment Specification on the SQA website will give you a great overview of the questions that could be asked. Read these carefully and make sure that there are no gaps in your knowledge and skills.

Make sure you know what to expect in the exam by having good knowledge of:

▶ how the exam paper is structured
▶ what type of questions will be asked
▶ how much time you should devote to each question
▶ which topics are your strongest and which are your weakest.

When planning your revision, you should make short summary notes from your textbook or course materials for each of your three topics. Remember to use memory aids such as mind-maps, flash cards and making notes in different-coloured ink. You should also practise skills-based questions.

Course components

Your final grade for Higher Modern Studies will be determined by three components. These are:

Component	Time	Marks
Question Paper 1	1 hour and 45 minutes	52
Question Paper 2	1 hour and 15 minutes	28
Assignment	Research period: 8 hours Production of evidence: 1 hour and 30 minutes	30

There is a total of 110 marks available. The marks you receive for the three assessments will be added together to determine your final grade.

The grade boundaries are:

▶ A = at least 77/110
▶ B = at least 66/110
▶ C = at least 55/110

The exam papers

Question paper 1

The first question paper requires you to answer one question from each of the three sections:

► Democracy in Scotland and the United Kingdom
► Social Issues in the United Kingdom
► International Issues

There are a number of different options within each section.

Section	Options	
Democracy in Scotland and the United Kingdom	• possible alternatives for the governance of Scotland • implications of the UK's decision to leave the European Union (EU) • effectiveness of parliamentary representatives in holding government to account • strengths and weaknesses of different electoral systems used in elections within the UK • factors which influence voting behaviour including class, age and media • ways in which citizens can influence government decision-making, including pressure groups	
Social issues in the United Kingdom	**Social inequality** • reasons why income and wealth inequality exists • reasons why health inequalities exist • effect of inequality on a group or groups in society • individualist and collectivist debate • effectiveness of measures taken to tackle inequalities, including government measures	**Crime and the law** • legal rights and responsibilities of UK citizens • causes and theories of crime • impact of crime on victims, offenders and their families • social and economic impact of crime on wider society • effectiveness of custodial and non-custodial responses to crime
International issues	**World power** • extent to which the political system allows democratic participation • political institutions and their ability to dominate government decision-making • socio-economic inequality and its impact on a specific group in society • effectiveness of government responses to socio-economic inequality • a world power's international influence	**World issues** • social, economic and political factors which have caused the issue • effects of the issue on individuals, families and communities • effects of the issue on the governments involved and the wider international community • effectiveness of individual countries in tackling the issue • effectiveness of international organisations in tackling the issue

There are three questions on this paper. You will answer **two** 20-mark questions and **one** 12-mark question. The focus of the 12-mark questions should alter from section to section each year. However, there is no guarantee of this.

The exam is 1 hour and 45 minutes. This means you should allow 40 minutes per 20-mark question and 25 minutes for the 12-mark question. Effective time management is essential, and by sticking to these timings you will give yourself the best chance of completing the full question paper. Practising timed essays at home is a good way of improving your time management and ensuring you know exactly how long you have got to cover each question.

The different question types

To what extent

To what extent is social class the most important factor in influencing voting behaviour? (20 marks)

Discuss

'Social class is the most important factor in influencing voting behaviour.' Discuss. (20 marks)

Evaluate

Evaluate the importance of social class in voting behaviour. (12 marks)

Analyse

Analyse the impact of social class on voting behaviour. (12 marks)

Question paper 2

The second question paper requires you to answer three questions by interpreting and using a number of sources provided by the SQA.

There are three types of question:

▶ An **objectivity** question, which involves detecting and explaining the degree of objectivity in the sources provided. This question is worth 10 marks.

▶ A **conclusion** question, which involves drawing and supporting complex conclusions using a range of sources. This question is worth 10 marks.

▶ A **reliability** question, where you must evaluate the reliability of a range of sources. This question is worth 8 marks.

You will have 1 hour and 15 minutes to attempt all three questions. This means you should spend 27 minutes on each 10-mark question, and 21 minutes on the 8-mark question.

This book will show you how to break down each of these questions and how to structure your answers effectively in order to maximise the marks and help you get the grade that you deserve.

All that is left to say is that we hope you enjoy the book and find it invaluable in steering you through Higher Modern Studies Question Papers 1 and 2. Do not let the book gather dust! Instead, allow it to be your constant revision companion and essential guide to doing very well in Higher Modern Studies.

Good luck!

KEY AREA INDEX GRID

Content	Practice Questions	Practice Paper A	Practice Paper B
Democracy in Scotland and the United Kingdom			
Alternatives for governance of Scotland			1a
Implications of decision to leave the EU		1b	
Effectiveness of parliamentary representatives	Exemplar		1b
Strengths and weaknesses of electoral systems	Exemplar	1c	1c
Ways of citizens to influence government decision-making		1a	
Factors which influence voting behaviour	Exemplar		
Social inequality			
Reasons why health inequalities exist	9	2b	
Effects of inequality on groups in society	13	8	2a
Individualist/collectivist viewpoint	3		2b
Effectiveness of measures to tackle inequalities	2	2a	
Crime and the law			
Legal rights and responsibilities			2c
Causes and theories of crime	4	2c	
Impact of crime on victims, offender and families	5		2d
Social and economic impact of crime on wider society	10		
Effectiveness of custodial and non-custodial responses to crime	14	2d	
World power			
Extent to which political systems allow democratic participation		3b	3b
Political institutions' ability to dominate decision-making	15		
Social-economic inequality on a specific group	11		3a
Effectiveness of government responses to socio-economic inequality	8		
International influence		3a	
World issues			
Social, economic and political causes of issue	6		3c
Effects of issue on individuals, families and communities	16	3c	
Effects of issue on governments involved and wider international community	12		3d
Effectiveness of individual countries in tackling issue Effectiveness of international organisations in tackling the issue	7	3d	

Practice makes permanent

This section of the book looks at the different question types you can expect to see on the exam papers. For each style of question, you will be given an example followed by the opportunity to answer a range of questions.

For Paper 1, you will need to demonstrate your in-depth knowledge of a particular topic, and your ability to analyse evidence, evaluate the information and come to a suitable conclusion, if required.

For Paper 2, you will demonstrate your skills of objectivity, drawing conclusions and evaluating the reliability of the sources.

Top Tip!

More marks are allocated for knowledge and understanding than skills, so it is important that you have a sound grasp of content.

Tips for success	Things to avoid
Answer the question as set and only provide information relevant to the question.	Do not turn the question into something it is not – you will not receive any marks for details or examples that are not relevant.
As far as you can, use up-to-date examples to illustrate your understanding of the question.	Do not provide answers that display limited analysis and/or evaluation.
Answer in detail and write in paragraphs with development of the points you wish to discuss.	Do not provide answers that are dated and too historical.
Show awareness of the difference between Analyse questions and Discuss/To what extent/Evaluate questions.	Do not provide answers that push together different issues, factors and explanations without development.
Ensure that your answer includes knowledge and understanding, analysis, evaluation, a structured and balanced line of argument and valid conclusions that refer to the question.	

Now let's take a closer look at the question types and see what you need to do to get full marks.

Paper 1

20-mark essay questions

>> HOW TO ANSWER

These questions begin with 'To what extent', or give you a statement to discuss. For example:

▶ To what extent is social class the most important factor in influencing the outcomes of elections? (20 marks)

▶ 'Social class is the most important factor in influencing the outcomes of elections.' Discuss. (20 marks)

SQA marking guidelines

Knowledge and understanding accounts for up to 8 marks. The remaining 12 marks are awarded for analysis and evaluation, and structured argument (6 marks for analysis and evaluation, 2 marks for an essay with a coherent line of argument, and 4 marks for making judgements and drawing relevant conclusions).

How can you achieve these marks?

Begin with a short introduction that highlights the key issues of the question and includes an outline of the content areas you should cover. This provides structure and the marker can follow your line of development.

You may wish to provide a sub-conclusion at the end of each content area – for example, a judgement on the effectiveness of committees to scrutinise government.

Your final conclusion will provide an overall judgement of the extent to which the viewpoint is correct.

You must structure your essay properly. You should include:

▶ an introduction that highlights the key issues of the question and includes an outline of the factors you will discuss – this provides structure and the marker can follow your line of argument

▶ in the main section of the essay, development of the factors highlighted in the introduction – you should provide relevant knowledge and examples to both support and question the viewpoint given. This will provide balance and an opportunity to provide analysis and evaluation

▶ a sub-conclusion for each of your paragraphs, if you wish

▶ a final conclusion which will provide an overall judgement of the extent to which the viewpoint is correct.

Look at the question below and see what you need to do to get full marks.

> **Top Tip!**
>
> In order to achieve top marks, you must write an answer that provides evidence for and against the statement, as well as an overall conclusion that considers the extent to which it is correct.

Marks allocation

For all of the worked examples in the Practice Questions section and marking instructions in the Practice Papers section, the following codes are used:

▶ K = Knowledge
▶ A = Analysis
▶ E = Evaluation
▶ S = Structure

'Some factors affecting voting behaviour are more influential than others.' Discuss.

Answer

Explanations of voting behaviour can be divided into short-term and long-term factors. Short-term factors cover issues such as the state of the economy, the image of the party leaders, the policies of the political parties and important issues of the day, such as Brexit. Public opinion on these issues can be shaped by the role of the media. Long-term factors cover the traditional explanations of social class, national identity, gender and religion. In this essay we will consider what are the most influential factors. **(1K)**

The media is one factor that influences voting behaviour. Newspapers are examples of traditional media that are allowed to be openly biased, which means they can try to influence their readers' political views. This can be seen in the most recent election where 79% of *Daily Telegraph* readers voted for the Conservatives and 68% of *Daily Mirror* readers voted for the Labour Party. **(1K)** This could show that newspapers influenced their readers to vote a certain way. This could highlight the link between newspaper readers and voting behaviour and could prove the effectiveness of the media in influencing their readers. Alternatively, it could show that people buy the newspapers that reflect their own opinions on issues such as political views. **(2A)**

With the rise of electronic media such as smartphones and the internet, newspapers' influence is decreasing. **(1K)** Thirty million UK citizens now have Facebook, and social media is becoming more influential with 50% of 18–24-year-olds stating that who they voted for was influenced by social media, which shows the influence of this type of media on how young people vote. It may be that young voters tend to be influenced by new media with older voters more likely to be swayed by older media, such as newspapers. **(1K 1A)**

However, older people are far more likely to vote than young people; and importantly, newspaper readership is far stronger among older people so its influence is still significant. **(1K)**

Social class is another factor that could influence how people vote, although it is not as influential as it used to be. The Conservatives tend to appeal to better-off middle-class voters, whereas those in poorer social groups such as C2, D and E are more likely to vote for Labour. **(1K)** This may be due to the types of policies of each party and who they are seen to traditionally represent. That said, the link is not as strong as it used to be, but still around 40% of voters vote according to their social class. However, social class is becoming less influential due to partisan de-alignment which means that people no longer vote for parties that represent their social class and are more likely to vote for parties based upon their own particular needs. **(2E)** Around 34% of voters consider themselves to be floating voters, which means they may switch who they vote for from election to election, depending upon party policies and their own individual choice. **(1K)**

The increase in the number of floating voters can also increase the influence of the media as these individuals can be swayed by the newspapers and websites. **(1A)**

Age can also be a factor in voting behaviour, particularly in terms of turnout. Voters over 60 years of age are twice as likely to turn out to vote than those under 35 years, which means that the results of elections are often decided by older voters. **(1K)** Certainly, there is evidence that the Scottish Independence vote and the Brexit vote were decided by older voters and the results could have been different if more younger people voted. **(1A)**

Therefore, we can see that there are many factors that can affect the outcome of elections, with age, social class and the media being influential. We should not overestimate the influence of the media as the SNP won a landslide election victory in the 2015 general election despite facing a hostile press. The Brexit divide in the UK has weakened the influence of social class and as such it is not as influential as it once was. **(1E)**

8K 5A 3E 2S = 18/20

Marker's commentary

This is a clear Grade A answer with a very sound structure (introduction and coverage of issues raised) worth 2 marks. The introduction outlines a wide range of factors and the main body of the essay considers some of the ones considered more important. Excellent balance is provided with sound analysis and evaluation of the factors covered. Some of the issues raised could have been expanded to provide greater depth.

You will find a C-grade answer for this question in the answer section, on page 18.

MARKS

Test your knowledge and understanding: 20-mark questions

Democracy in Scotland and the United Kingdom

1 'Some factors affecting voting behaviour are more influential than others.' Discuss.   20

Social issues in the United Kingdom: Social inequality

2 'Government policies introduced to tackle inequality have been successful.' Discuss.   20

3 To what extent should it be the Government's and not the individual's responsibility to tackle inequality?   20

Social issues in the United Kingdom: Crime and the law

4 To what extent are some theories of crime more influential than others?   20

5 'Crime can impact on many different groups.' Discuss.   20

International issues: World issues

6 'Some factors are more important than others in causing the world issue you have studied.' Discuss.   20

7 To what extent have international organisations been effective at tackling terrorism?   20

International issues: World power

8 To what extent has the world power you have studied been effective in tackling social inequalities?   20

12-mark essay questions

>> HOW TO ANSWER

In your exam you will answer one question worth 12 marks. These questions ask you to evaluate or analyse.

The evaluation question requires you to compare the factor noted in the question with other factors you know to be relevant. The analysis question requires you to focus solely on the factor specified in the question.

SQA marking guidelines

Knowledge and understanding accounts for up to 8 marks. The remaining 4 marks are awarded for analysis or evaluation. If you make more analytical/evaluative points than necessary to gain the maximum of 4 marks, these can be credited as knowledge and understanding marks, as long as they meet the criteria for this.

How can you achieve these marks?
Evaluation question

To answer evaluation questions effectively, you need to:

▶ make judgements based on criteria
▶ draw conclusions on the extent to which a view is supported by the evidence

Top Tip!

For a 12-mark essay a very brief introduction or scene-setting is all that is required, and for an analysis question a brief conclusion is not necessary. There are no marks for structure.

- offer counter-arguments, including possible alternative interpretations
- consider the overall impact or significance of all factors
- consider the relative importance of factors in relation to the context.

Analysis question

To answer an analysis question well, you need to:

- demonstrate your understanding of the issue
- identify numerous parts to the issue
- show your understanding of how these parts affect each other, and the issue as a whole
- identify the likely consequences.

The two types of question look similar, but they must be answered differently. For example:

- Evaluate the importance of the media on voting behaviour. (12 marks)
- Analyse the influence of the media on voting behaviour. (12 marks)

In the **evaluation question** you will not just cover the role of the media in influencing voting behaviour, but of other influences such as social class, party policies and images of political leaders. You need to make an **evaluative** judgement on how important the media is in comparison to other factors.

In the **analysis question** you will **only** cover the role of the media in influencing voting behaviour. You will concentrate on the influences of different aspects of the media, such as newspapers, television and new media.

Evaluation question worked example

Let's look at the worked example below to show you how to answer an 'evaluate' question.

Evaluate the effectiveness of Parliament in holding the Government to account.

Answer 1

The main role of Parliament is to hold the Government to account. There are a number of ways in which they can do this. Some methods are more effective than others.

One way that Parliament holds the UK Government to account is through Select Committees. These are groups of MPs who come together to scrutinise the work of Government around various issues such as education, finance or defence. A committee can call up members of the Government and ask them to answer questions regarding their department. **(1K)** Committees can also call experts or members of the public to answer questions. They can also make suggestions regarding policy. **(1K)** This can be effective as it makes ministers answerable for their actions. Also, around 40% of their suggestions end up being included in Acts of Parliament. **(1E)** However, the Government can also choose to ignore or disregard what the committees recommend, which shows that they are not that effective. **(1E)**

Another way that Parliament holds the Government to account is during Question Time, or Prime Minister's Question Time, which occurs weekly and gives the leader of the opposition and backbench MPs the chance to put the PM or Ministers on the spot. **(1K)** This can be effective as it has the potential to publicly embarrass the PM and make them look ineffective, weak or incompetent. **(1E)** Jeremy Corbyn has managed to do this a number of times recently over the PM's handling of Brexit. **(1K)** However, it can be seen to be ineffective as it often ends up being a shouting match with little progress being made. Also, the Government sometimes plant questions with sympathetic MPs, which can waste time and limits its effectiveness. **(1E)**

Voting after debates is another way that MPs can hold the Government to account. They can vote against government proposals or bills and criticise the Government's handling of a situation. **(1K)** The effectiveness can depend upon the size of government majority that they have. The larger a majority, the more difficult it is for the Government to be defeated. However, the smaller a majority, the easier it is to defeat the Government. **(1E)** This can be seen in the way that Parliament rejected PM May's proposals for leaving the EU. **(1K)** The Parliament rejected her proposals every time she presented them. This led to her resigning. This really shows how effective Parliament can be. **(1E)**

6K 6E = 12/12

The candidate gives three detailed paragraphs and points about how Parliament can hold Government to account. These are knowledgeable, relevant and creditworthy. Some good use of analysis in this answer backs up and adds value to the insightful knowledge points made.

Read Answer 2 and see what you could do to improve it.

Analysis question worked example

Let's look at the worked example below to show you how to answer an 'analyse' question.

With reference to a voting system you have studied, analyse the extent the voting system provides for fair representation.

Answer

One voting system I have studied is the Additional Member System (AMS). This system provides for fair representation because it is more representative of smaller parties. AMS allows for voters to have two votes – one for a party and one for a candidate. This gives AMS a proportional element, meaning that the overall result is a direct link to the percentage of votes cast for all parties. This means that if a party gets roughly 15% of the votes, they will get roughly 15% of the seats, which helps smaller parties, such as the Green Party, who won seats in the Scottish Parliament due to AMS. **(2K)** This shows a fairer representation as it does not just benefit the two larger parties, but instead benefits all of the parties. **(1A)**

However, sometimes AMS can lead to a coalition, which can mean that smaller parties become more powerful than they should be as they could end up in government despite only winning a small number of seats. This happened in the Scottish Parliament when Labour joined in government with the Lib Dems. Many felt that this was unfair as the Lib Dems finished in fourth place but ended up in government. **(1K)** This means that the system can be seen to be undemocratic as they had more power than they should have. **(1A)**

Therefore, AMS can provide fair representation as it means that smaller parties are being represented fairly. However, this can be unrepresentative as it can give smaller parties more power than they deserve. **(1A)**

Another way that AMS can provide fair representation is that it can mean that more females and ethnic minorities are represented in Parliament. This is because with AMS voters get to choose a party on the ballot paper as their regional MSP. **(1K)** Parties choose which candidates represent the region, and some parties deliberately pick women or ethnic minorities as their candidates. In the Scottish Parliament, over 35% of candidates are women, compared to only around 29% in Westminster. **(1K)** This shows that AMS can lead to more women being elected into Parliament. **(1A)**

One way that AMS can be seen to be unrepresentative or not providing fair representation is that it can often result in a coalition government which no one actually voted for and which ends up creating compromise policies that may not be popular with the voters or they may not have had a full say on whether they wanted them or not. **(1A)**

Also, while it provides fairer representation than First Past the Post (FPTP), it is not perfect. In the 2016 Scottish Parliament elections, the Liberal Democrats received around 115,000 votes and gained only one seat, in contrast to the Greens, whose 150,000 votes won six regional seats. **(1K 1A)**

6K 6A = 12/12

The candidate shows a good level of knowledge with regard to how the voting system works including an element of proportionality. They give strong creditworthy knowledge and consistently make analytical comments which are creditworthy.

MARKS

Test your knowledge and understanding: 'Evaluate' questions

Social issues in the United Kingdom: Social inequality

9 Evaluate the causes of health inequalities. **12**

Social issues in the United Kingdom: Crime and the law

10 Evaluate the social and economic impact of crime. **12**

International issues: World power

11 Evaluate the impact that inequality has on a specific group that you have studied. **12**

International issues: World issues

12 Evaluate the impact of the world issue you have studied on governments. **12**

Test your knowledge and understanding: 'Analysis' questions

Social issues in the United Kingdom: Social inequality

13 With reference to a group you have studied, analyse the impact of inequality on that group. **12**

Social issues in the United Kingdom: Crime and the law

14 Analyse the effectiveness of custodial sentences. **12**

International issues: World power

15 Analyse the powers of the executive branch of government. **12**

International issues: World issues

16 Analyse the impact that the world issue you have studied has had on individuals affected by the issue. **12**

Paper 2

>> HOW TO ANSWER

Paper 2 contains questions that require you to evaluate the sources provided.

There are three questions on Paper 2.

- ▶ Question 1 is an **objectivity** question. This involves detecting and explaining the degree of objectivity in the sources provided. This question is worth 10 marks.
- ▶ Question 2 is a **conclusion** question. This involves drawing and supporting complex conclusions using a range of sources. This question is worth 10 marks.
- ▶ Question 3 is a **reliability** question. You must evaluate the reliability of a range of sources. This question is worth 8 marks.

Tips for success	Things to avoid
▶ Only use the sources provided. ▶ Use **all** the sources provided. ▶ Link evidence from the different sources to give a detailed argument. ▶ Interpret any statistical evidence to show how it links to the question being asked.	▶ Do not state your own knowledge or opinion on the topic. ▶ Do not just rely on one piece of evidence from a source to provide argument. ▶ Do not just repeat the statistics without interpreting and explaining them.

Objectivity questions (10 marks)

>> HOW TO ANSWER

SQA marking guidelines

- ▶ You can gain up to 3 marks for a single developed point, depending on use of evidence and the quality of the analysis or evaluation.
- ▶ Marks are awarded where candidates synthesise information both within and between sources. For full marks, you must refer to all sources in your answer.
- ▶ There is a maximum of **8 marks** if no overall judgement is made on extent of accuracy of the statement.

How can you achieve these marks?

- ▶ You should provide around three arguments to **support** the statement, linking evidence from both within and between sources.
- ▶ You should then provide around three arguments to **oppose** the statement from both within and between sources.
- ▶ You must provide an overall conclusion to explain the extent to which the statement is correct.

Look at the question on the next page and see what you need to do to get full marks.

Top Tip!

Your overall conclusion should say the statement is correct to a (very) large extent or to a (very) limited extent and give evidence. Do not say something is totally correct/incorrect.

17 Study Sources A, B and C then attempt the question that follows.

SOURCE A

A surprise outcome in the 2016 USA presidential election

All of the opinion polls predicted that Hillary Clinton, the Democrat candidate, would win the USA presidential election. However, to the shock of most Americans, Donald Trump, the Republican candidate, gained a clear victory in the Electoral College, winning 306 votes compared to Clinton's 232. This surprise result made his victory appear outstanding.

The President of the USA is not chosen directly by the American people. Instead, presidents are elected by 'electors' who are chosen by popular vote on a state-by-state basis.

These 'electors' then award their states' Electoral College votes to the candidate with the greatest support in their state. The two major political parties are the Democratic Party and the Republican Party. There are other political parties that participate in presidential elections, and in 2016 several other presidential candidates took part. In total these candidates gained about 5% of the votes.

The number of Electoral College votes in each state depends on the size of the state. For example, Florida, which has a large population (19.5 m), receives 29 Electoral College votes compared to the three received by Vermont, which has a small population (0.6 m). There are 538 Electoral College votes in total. However, the popular votes achieved in a state are not shared proportionally between the leading candidates. In the 2016 presidential election in Florida, Donald Trump won 49.1% of the popular vote compared to 47.8% for Hillary Clinton, yet Trump received all of the 29 Electoral College votes.

The key to victory in the Electoral College is to win as many 'swing states' as possible (many states are either solid Democrat or Republican, and swing states are those where either candidate could win). In the 2016 election, Hillary Clinton won only one of the five key swing states. It was a close result in several of these swing states – Trump's combined lead in Florida, Michigan, Pennsylvania and Wisconsin was only 100,000 votes.

Yet Hillary Clinton won the most popular votes (the total number of votes each candidate received across the country). Clinton received 65.5 million votes compared to 62.8 million votes for Trump.

Clinton's support among non-whites was lower than Obama received in 2012. However, she still won 88% of the black vote and 71% of Hispanic and Asian votes. Trump's main support came from the rich, and from poorly educated white voters, including women and those aged over 64. The gender vote was complicated, with unmarried women favouring Clinton by 62% to 33% and white married women favouring Trump by 53% to 43%. The turnout was only 55.6% compared to 57.5% in 2012.

SOURCE B

Voting by gender, income, ethnicity, age and education in the 2016 presidential election (%)

	Trump	Clinton
Gender		
Male	53	41
Female	42	54
Income		
Earning less than $40,000	41	53
Earning more than $40,000	49	47
Ethnicity		
White non-Hispanic	58	37
Hispanic	21	74
African American	8	88
Age		
18–44	40	52
Over 45	53	44
Education		
Non-college-educated white	67	27
College-educated white	49	45

SOURCE C

USA presidential results 2016 and 2012: Popular vote (%) and Electoral College (%)

Party and candidate	Popular vote 2016	Popular vote 2012
Democrat: Clinton	48.1	51.0
Republican: Trump	46.2	47.1
Party and candidate	**Electoral College 2016**	**Electoral College 2012**
Democrat: Clinton	43.2	61.7
Republican: Trump	56.8	38.3

Note: Obama was the Democrat candidate and Romney was the Republican candidate in the 2012 presidential election.

Attempt the following question, using only the information in Sources A, B and C.

To what extent is it accurate to state that the result of the 2016 USA Presidential Election was 'an outstanding victory for Donald Trump'?

Answer 1

Evidence to support the viewpoint:

It was an outstanding victory as all of the opinion polls predicted a Clinton victory and this is also reflected in the Electoral College results (Source A).

Evidence to oppose the viewpoint:

It was not an outstanding result as Clinton won more popular votes than Trump – 65.5 million compared to 62.8 million for Trump (Source A).

Overall conclusion:

The statement is completely untrue as the majority did not vote for him.

Marker's commentary

This is a poor answer as the student fails to use all of the sources and does not link up evidence within and between sources. The overall conclusion is not acceptable as it is not balanced.

Overall: 2/8 (Fail).

Answer 2

Evidence to support the viewpoint:

It was an outstanding victory as all of the opinion polls predicted a Clinton victory and this is also reflected in the Electoral College results. Trump won a commanding 306 votes compared to 232 for Clinton (Source A).

Evidence to oppose the viewpoint:

It was not an outstanding result as Clinton won more popular votes than Trump – 65.5 million compared to 62.8 million for Trump (Source A). In fact Trump's popular vote as a percentage was lower than what Romney (the Republican candidate) achieved In 2012 – Romney won 47.1% compared to 46.2% for Trump.

Overall conclusion:

To a large extent it was not an outstanding victory as many groups in society did not vote for Trump.

Marker's commentary

This is a better answer as the student uses information within and between sources to support the different viewpoints, with each of the first two paragraphs gaining 2 marks each. The student also provides an overall conclusion but provides no evidence to support the statement (so 1/2).

Overall: 5/10 (Grade C).

To improve to a Grade A answer you will need to use more evidence from the sources to support and oppose the viewpoint, and to provide evidence to support your overall conclusion.

Now, over to you to complete a Grade A answer for the above question. The marking instructions for this question are on page 37.

Conclusion questions (10 marks)

>> HOW TO ANSWER

SQA marking guidelines

▶ You can gain up to 3 marks for a single developed point, depending on use of evidence and the quality of the analysis or evaluation.

▶ Marks are awarded where candidates synthesise information from both within and between sources. For full marks, you must refer to all sources in your answer.

▶ There is a maximum of **8 marks** if no overall conclusion is provided.

How can you gain these marks?

▶ You must first draw conclusions about three sub-statements, linking evidence from both within and between sources.

▶ For each sub-statement, you should first provide a conclusion and then provide evidence to support your conclusion.

▶ You must provide an overall conclusion to answer the question's final statement.

Look at the question below and see what you need to do to get full marks.

18 Study Sources A, B and C below then attempt the question that follows.

> **Top Tip!**
>
> A surprising number of students fail to provide an accurate overall conclusion. You should read the final statement carefully, as it will be different from the three sub-statements.

SOURCE A

A careful examination of the socio-economic distribution of people in Britain who are overweight or obese confirms that fat is a poverty/class issue. The lowest social class, who experience extreme poverty, has levels of obesity that match American levels, whereas the highest and wealthiest social classes have the lowest obesity levels.

A 2014 Scottish report on the body mass index (BMI) of Primary 1 children who started school in 2012 highlighted the disparity between those in the richest and poorest areas of Scotland. Children classified as obese were twice as likely to be from areas of deprivation. Chris Mantle, a member of the Association for Nutrition, stated, 'The data shows us that sadly as deprivation increases, healthy weight declines'.

A 2016 NHS Scotland report indicates that the number of Primary 1 obese children has decreased slightly, but also indicates the strong link between deprivation and obesity. The decrease can be explained in a decline in the number of overweight and obese children from more affluent areas; unfortunately, there has been no decline in the proportion of children from deprived areas experiencing overweight and obesity issues.

Recent international studies by the McKinsey Global Institute highlight the general obesity problems faced by both Scotland and the UK. Both Scotland and England are in the top ten OECD countries experiencing high overweight and obesity levels, with Scotland experiencing obesity levels of 27% of the general public and the UK 25%.

Numerous health surveys in England suggest that women with no or poor school examination qualifications suffer more from obesity than men. This is the group most likely to experience poverty. However, the group with the lowest level of obesity is poor men and rich women, which contradicts the view that the sole explanation is poverty.

Figures released in July 2019 by the National Records of Scotland highlight that Scotland, based on population size, has the highest level of drug-related deaths in Europe. Drug use and related deaths is 17 times higher in Scotland's poorest areas compared to the wealthiest areas. The locations with the worst rates are Dundee (NHS Tayside), Glasgow and the towns of Greenock and Port Glasgow – all areas of high deprivation. In contrast, the locations with the lowest rates are in more rural areas such as parts of NHS Grampian, Borders and Shetland – all wealthier areas of Scotland.

The number of drug-related deaths has trebled over the last 20 years and is almost three times higher than the figures in England.

SOURCE B

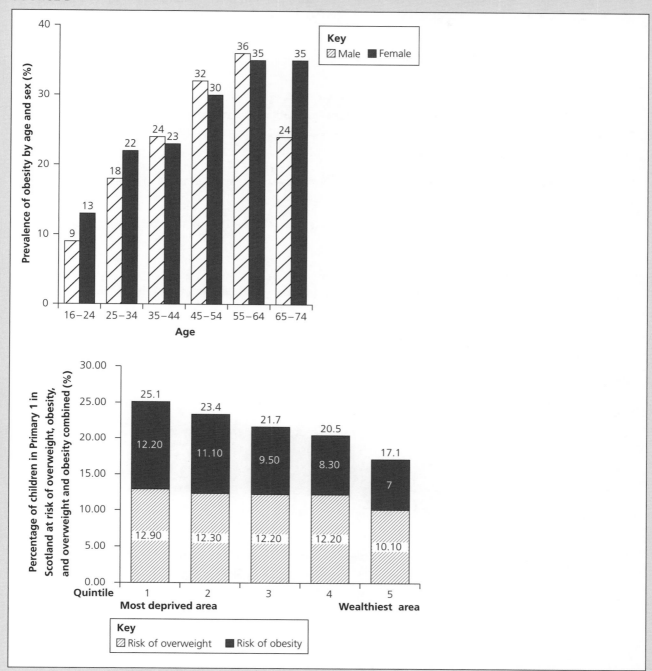

SOURCE C

Drug-related deaths in Scotland, selected years

1996	244
2000	292
2005	336
2010	485
2015	706
2017	934
2018	1,187

Drug-related deaths per 1000 population, selected NHS board areas, average for 2014–18

Ayrshire and Arran	0.17
Borders	0.12
Grampian	0.12
Tayside	0.18
Greater Glasgow and Clyde	0.23
Shetland	0.07

Attempt the following question, using **only** the information in Sources A, B and C.

What conclusions can be drawn about the levels of obesity in the UK?

You must draw one conclusion about each of the following:

▶ the link between weight issues and income
▶ the link between weight issues and gender
▶ the link between drug-related deaths and income.

You must give an overall conclusion about the trend in drug abuse in Scotland.

Conclusion 1

The link between weight issues and income

Conclusion: There is a clear link between poverty and those who experience weight issues.

Marker's commentary

A conclusion is given for this answer. It fails to provide supporting evidence and so gains no marks.

Conclusion 2

The link between weight issues and income

Conclusion: There is a clear link between poverty and those who experience weight issues including obesity.

This is supported in Source A which indicates that the lowest social classes have the highest levels of obesity.

Marker's commentary

A conclusion is given for this answer with limited supporting evidence. This student would be awarded 1 mark. It needs more evidence to support the statement.

So, what do you need to do to gain 3 marks? Make use of the evidence provided to make an evaluative comment, as outlined below.

Conclusion 3

The link between weight issues and income

Conclusion: There is a clear link between poverty and those children who experience weight issues, including obesity.

This is supported in Source A, which shows that Scottish children from the poorest areas of Scotland are twice as likely to be obese compared to children from the wealthiest areas. This is further supported in Source C, which shows that among Primary 1 pupils there is a clear contrast between those living in areas of poverty compared to those in the least deprived or wealthiest areas – 12% of children in the most deprived areas are obese compared to 7% in the wealthiest areas, a significant difference.

Marker's commentary

This student links detailed evidence from two sources and also provides evaluative comment, and achieves the maximum of 3 marks.

Now write your own answer to the question above. The marking instructions for this question are on page 38.

Reliability questions (8 marks)

>> HOW TO ANSWER

SQA marking guidelines

▶ You can gain up to 2 marks for a single developed point, depending on use of evidence and the quality of the analysis or evaluation.

▶ For full marks, you must refer to all sources in your answer.

▶ You must make a judgement based on the evidence of the most reliable source.

▶ If you do not provide an overall judgement, the maximum you can achieve is 6 marks.

▶ If you only consider one factor, for example the date of the three sources, then you will only achieve a maximum of 3 marks.

How can you achieve these marks?

You should take each source in turn and outline its strength and weakness in terms of reliability. Then you should decide which source is the most reliable and justify your choice.

19 Study Sources A, B and C then attempt the question that follows.

Top Tip!

Consider:

• Date of source – are the points up to date? Is the Information still valid and reliable?

• Objectivity – is the author presenting just their own viewpoint? Are any of their comments factual?

• Opinion polls – is the sample valid?

SOURCE A

Interview with British jihadi in Syria

What made you leave the UK? What was the deciding factor?

To come to Syria. To leave *dar al kufr* [the land of disbelievers].

Why are you out in Syria?

To spread the religion of Allah and to help Muslims. I can speak Arabic and English. That's like my only skill. I've spent efforts to take down the Syrian government. That's all I want to say.

Have you joined ISIS?

I'm not ISIS, but I believe in the Sharia. I believe we should follow Islam how the first Muslims did. I also think that whatever I say, the media will probably freestyle with it and make up more nicknames for me as a result of the void they have in their lives.

What do you think about ISIS? Can you give us an insight into what's going on in Syria with ISIS? They've recently released a video saying they'll attack the UK – what are your thoughts on that?

I'm doing my own thing. I don't focus that much on what ISIS does. Also, this may sound strange but this is genuinely the first time someone's told me they threatened to attack the UK, which is probably a bit embarrassing, seeing as I'm in Syria and you'd expect I'd hear these things. If Britain stopped bombing Muslims in Syria the Muslims in Syria would stop attacking them. Is that hard to understand?

Source: The Independent, '"Jihadi Jack" Letts interview: Former Oxford schoolboy calls on British people to convert to Islam as he brands David Cameron an "evil creature"', by Shehab Khan, published 30 January 2016.

SOURCE B

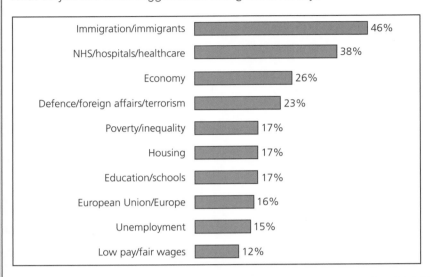

Public opinion survey: issues facing Britain

What do you see as the biggest issue facing the UK today?

Issue	%
Immigration/immigrants	46%
NHS/hospitals/healthcare	38%
Economy	26%
Defence/foreign affairs/terrorism	23%
Poverty/inequality	17%
Housing	17%
Education/schools	17%
European Union/Europe	16%
Unemployment	15%
Low pay/fair wages	12%

Source: Ipsos MORI interviewed a representative quota sample of 1,011 adults aged 18+ across Great Britain, 7–20 January 2016.

SOURCE C

Source: Channel 4 News website, 'Do we know why we are in Afghanistan?', by Jon Snow, published 28 July 2009.

Attempt the following question, using only the information in Sources A, B and C.

To what extent are Sources A, B and C reliable?

You must provide an overall conclusion on the most reliable source of information.

Answer 1

Source A is not reliable as it was published before 2019.

Marker's commentary

This student provides an unrealistic reason for it being unreliable and is awarded no marks.

Answer 2

Source A is largely reliable and trustworthy. It has been published by a quality UK newspaper, The Independent.

Marker's commentary

This student concentrates on the source of the extract and explains why it is trustworthy. This answer would gain 1 mark.

So, what would you need to do to improve this answer?

Answer 3

Source A is largely reliable and trustworthy. It has been published by a quality UK newspaper, The Independent. We are aware that the interview is biased as it is the views of a British jihadi. We can assume that the journalist, Shehab Khan, will follow journalistic ethics and standards when writing this article.

Marker's commentary

This student provides a detailed analysis of the source and would gain 2 marks.

Now write your own answer to the question above.

Once you are finished you can go to page 39 to compare your own answer to the marking instructions.

Paper 1

Test your knowledge and understanding: 20-mark questions

Democracy in Scotland and the United Kingdom

1 'Some factors affecting voting behaviour are more influential than others.' Discuss.

Grade C response

One factor that can influence voting is the media and newspapers. The media can be influential as it can be seen as an easy way to gain people's attention during elections. Newspapers tend to be read by older voters and are therefore more likely to affect how they vote than younger voters. **(1K)** Newspapers can be biased in favour of political parties, such as the *Daily Mail* supporting the Conservatives and *The National* supporting the SNP. Many people tend to buy papers which support their own view and will not be influenced as their minds may already be made up – for example a buyer of *The National* is already likely to support Independence or the SNP and would vote that way in elections. **(2K)**

Social class is another factor. How much people earn and where they live dictates the social class they are likely to be in. It can also affect how they vote. A well-off person in a rural English constituency is more likely to vote Conservative compared to someone in a poorly paid job who lives in Glasgow. **(1K)** They are more likely to vote Labour or SNP. Therefore, the social class you are in can influence who you vote for. **(1A)** However, the link between voting and social class is not as strong as it used to be. There are more floating voters now who change preference from election to election, meaning that the link between social class and voting is not as strong as it used to be. **(1E)**

Social media is a growing influence on how people vote nowadays. It is a really influential short-term factor, with apps such as Facebook and Twitter a way for politicians to try to influence how people vote, particularly among young voters, but young people are less likely to vote than older voters so its influence might be limited, particularly as seen in the Brexit vote. **(1K 1A)**

Overall, some factors are more important that others, with short-term factors such as social media more important than social class. **(1E)**

5K 2A 2E 1S = 10/20

Marker's commentary

The candidate gains some credit for points about social class and social media and there is some good insight shown with regard to readership of newspapers and who they are likely to vote for, but for a 20-mark answer there needs to much more in terms of points made, discussion and examples as well as analysis and evaluation.

Grade A response

See pages 2–3 for a Grade A response.

Social issues in the United Kingdom: Social inequality

2 'Government policies introduced to tackle inequality have been successful.' Discuss.

Grade C response

The Government have introduced many policies to tackle inequalities. One thing the Scottish Government have done is to introduce free prescriptions and eye tests. This is to ensure that poverty is not a barrier to receiving medical care or experiencing good health. This is only in place in Scotland, but has proven to be fairly successful. **(1K, 1A)** Health statistics show that Scots are living a little bit longer and that, in some cases, our health is improving. This shows that by making prescriptions free, it can benefit the overall health of the nation. **(1A)**

Another policy introduced to tackle inequalities includes a broad range of anti-tobacco and anti-smoking measures. Since 2006, the Scottish Government have introduced a wide variety of policies, including a ban on smoking in public places, plain packaging for cigarettes, cigarettes being out of sight in shops, as well as a ban on smoking in a car if there is a child under 16 present. **(2K)** These measures were introduced due to Scotland's really poor rates of respiratory illnesses and early deaths due to smoking-related illnesses. **(1K)**

Since these have been introduced there has been a reduction in the overall number of smokers as well as some positive health statistics, particularly in the areas of lung cancers, heart attacks and strokes. This shows that these policies have had some success in making Scottish people cut down on cigarettes and it has benefited them due to better health. **(1K 1E)**

The introduction of minimum unit pricing has also led to a reduction in consumption of alcohol, particularly among those in social groups C2, D and E. This has also led to a reduction in hospital admissions caused by over-consumption of alcohol. This shows that governments can improve the lives of their people by some of the policies they introduce. **(1K 1E)**

6K 2A 2E 1S = 11/20

Marker's commentary

The candidate has attempted to answer the question, but it is fairly light on content and knowledge. Their points are accurate and worth some marks, but for a 20-mark essay the candidate needs to cover at least four separate points in detail with up-to-date examples that have analysis and evaluation that is linked back to the question.

Grade A response

The Government have introduced many policies in an attempt to tackle gender inequalities, some of which have been more effective than others. Some of these policies include: The Equality Act 2010, National Minimum Wage/National Living Wage/Tax Credits/benefit cuts, the Equality and Human Rights Commission and Work of Equal Value. To evaluate their success, each of these factors will be examined.

There are many reasons to show that government policies have been effective in tackling gender inequality. It is now illegal to discriminate against women in the workplace. If they feel that they have been discriminated against, then they can take their employer to court. **(1K)** This shows that it could be argued that there are now many more legal rights than ever before. **(1A)** If women feel that they have been discriminated against and want help initially, they can turn to the Equality and Human Rights Commission (EHRC) who will give them advice and legal support about how to take the case forward. **(1K)**

Companies and organisations such as local councils and the police need to produce figures and information every year regarding their gender pay gap, the percentage of male and female workers as well as the types of jobs they do. **(1K)** Men get paid more than women for doing similar types of jobs, such as a school janitor will get paid more than a school cleaner for doing similar types of work. Many councils have had to pay millions of pounds to the women who were poorly paid throughout their work. The average pay-out is about £30,000, but some were paid £100,000. **(2K)** This shows that the Equality Act 2010 has been successful in tackling inequality as women are now receiving compensation from the councils where they were employed. **(1A)**

Overall, government policies have been effective, as 1.5 million female workers benefited because of the National Minimum Wage. Overnight, 2 million workers saw an increase in their wages, with 1.5 million of those being women. **(1K)** This benefited women more than men as women are more likely to work in lower-paid jobs. **(1A)** The gender pay gap is narrowing; however, women still earn less than men. Also, many women are now breaking through the 'glass ceiling' in specific types of employment, such as business. **(1K)** This shows that women are being successful in tackling discrimination and are fighting for equality, but they have a long way to go to achieve it. **(1A)**

Despite legislation such as the 2010 Equality Act, 30,000 women are sacked every year because they are pregnant. The gender pay gap still exists in many workplaces – for example a 22% gap within the BBC and 35% in the *Daily Telegraph*. **(2K)** Sexual harassment and discrimination still take place in the workplace. However, campaigns such as the MeToo and TimesUp campaigns attempt to tackle this discrimination against women and show that this is still an issue within the workplace. Many of the top jobs are still dominated by men and it is very hard for everyone to break the 'glass ceiling'. **(2K)** This shows that there is still a great deal of progress to be made when tackling inequalities. **(1E)**

The benefit cuts have had a huge impact on women. This is because women are more likely to be poor and use benefits – 85% of lone-parent households are headed up by females. **(1A)** This affects their ability to work full time and the earnings they receive. Poor women are paying the price of benefit cuts. On average, lone-parent families will lose £50 per week. **(1K)** Government policies in the last decade have made it more difficult to achieve gender equality and show that inequalities still exist and government policies may have made things worse rather than better. **(1E)**

In conclusion, equality between the genders is improving but inequality still exists, and it is negatively impacting women. As more things change, the more they seem to stay the same. Maybe the law needs to be 'toughened up' to put pressure on these companies into producing these reports and to make it more difficult to 'wriggle out' of things. However, women are successfully breaking through the 'glass ceiling' and tackling sexism and discrimination in the workplace. **(1E)**

12K (capped at 8) 4A 2E 2S = 16/20

Marker's commentary

A thorough response with a good exhibition of knowledge about the question topic that scores the maximum for knowledge (8 marks). The candidate makes some good analysis and evaluation, but these sections are the weakest sections. A little bit more by way of analysis and evaluation would turn a really good A response into a full-marks response.

---

3   To what extent should it be the Government's and not the individual's responsibility to tackle inequality?

Note: this additional guidance for 'Social issues in the United Kingdom: Social inequality' provides a Grade A response only.

Grade A response

A collectivist is someone who believes that the Government should provide and meet the needs of those who most need it – for example, the sick, poor, unemployed and elderly. Political parties, such as the SNP or Corbyn's Labour, are collectivists. The Welfare State and the NHS are examples of collectivism. Individualists are people who believe that the Government should not intervene in helping people. Theresa May, David Cameron and the Conservatives tend to be more individualist. Many people believe that the Government should tackle social inequality, but many believe it is down to the individual. **(2K)**

The smoking ban and other smoking-related policies of the Scottish Parliament have led to many people giving it up. The number of heart attacks caused by smoking has dropped to 17%. This shows that the collectivist Government is working, as we are becoming healthier and living longer. **(1K 1E)** Minimum unit pricing (MUP) has made alcohol more expensive, and it is hoped that this will help reduce the number of alcohol-related illnesses. This also shows that collectivism is the way forward if you want to live a healthy life. The National Minimum Wage helped 2 million workers, 75% of which were female. This encourages people to find work and supports the idea that work pays. **(2K)**

In Scotland, the SNP Government are collectivist and have introduced a whole range of policies to make Scotland healthier and wealthier, such as free prescriptions, free bus passes for the over-60s, free tuition fees and cancer screening checks, as well as maintaining EMA to encourage young people to stay on at school. **(1K)** This shows that because the Scottish Parliament have the devolved power of health, they can take control of health issues arising in the country and can help tackle them early before they cause major problems. **(1A)** Overall, it is clear that government action works. Collectivist action tends to improve our well-being in areas such as health, where inequality exists, and has made a massive difference in people's lives. They are living longer, are healthier and have a better standard of living. Therefore, collectivism works. **(1E)**

Collectivists argue that inequalities are too wide to leave to the individual, and that health and wealth inequalities are far too big to leave to the individual. For example, in Glasgow the male life expectancy is 70, but in Bearsden it is almost 80. This suggests that they would need the intervention of the Government to tackle this effectively, and to take control. The Government are best placed to control the Welfare State. This is evidence that only the Government can deliver the aims of the Welfare State, that it takes government action in order to create fairness and equality in society. **(1K 1E)**

When looking at health inequalities, Scotland has a poorer health record than England. Scotland is poorer, there are more people in poverty. Glasgow also has worse health inequalities than Edinburgh and is poorer. **(1K)** This shows that poverty equals poorer health, and only government action can effectively tackle this problem. However, things are improving. Fewer people are smoking and more people are giving up due to the smoking ban and other policies. **(1E)** Fewer young people are getting drunk at the weekend because the Scottish Government have health campaigns encouraging people to drink less. Scotland's bowel and cervical cancer rates are among the highest in Europe. The Scottish Government want to tackle this issue, and now have Well Man clinics encouraging men to talk and go to their doctor. **(1K)** This shows that problems are too big for individuals to deal with themselves as they need to be encouraged by government policies and campaigns to take action for their own health. **(1A)**

However, it is argued that we are individuals who should take responsibility for our own health and well-being. Many inequalities are created by people not taking responsibility for themselves. People make poor lifestyle choices that create inequality in society. The big three killers in Scotland are heart attacks, cancers and strokes, which can all be attributed to some degree to poor lifestyle choices. No one forces people to smoke, no one forces people to drink, no one forces people to eat unhealthily or not take exercise. No amount of government campaigns will change the way that some people make poor choices. People can change if they want to. **(1K 1E)** This shows that individuals must take responsibility for their own inequalities. Poor people tend to make poorer lifestyle choices, so in many ways they are victims of their own poor lifestyle choices. There is a clear link between poverty, poor lifestyle choices and inequality. **(2A)** These links can be shown by the Equally Well Report and Working Together for a Healthier Scotland. **(1K)** Even allowing for poor lifestyle choices, those in lower social groups are more likely to suffer employment and health inequalities. **(1E)**

In conclusion, the Government are best placed to tackle inequality as they are the only ones that can create laws such as the Equality Act, smoking ban, National Minimum Wage, etc. However, many inequalities are created through personal choice and people could perhaps do more to tackle their own health inequalities by making better and healthier lifestyle choices, such as stopping smoking, drinking in moderation, eating healthily and taking exercise. **(1E)**

8K (capped at 8) 4A 6E 2S = 20/20

Marker's commentary

This is a very accomplished essay from the candidate. They clearly know what the question focus is and have lots of knowledge about the issue to share with the marker. They make many knowledge points throughout the essay and use these knowledge points and relevant examples to create analysis points and evaluative comment throughout the essay. They score very highly due to this and it is clearly a full-mark 20/20 attempt.

Social issues in the United Kingdom: Crime and the law

4   To what extent are some theories of crime more influential than others?

Grade C response

One theory regarding the causes of crime comes from Lombroso who believed that physical appearance and biological factors are the main causes. He believed that the size of someone's nose or body shape was an indicator of their likelihood to commit crime. His theory was from the nineteenth century and has been discounted and disproved by other theories. **(1K)** However, there can be a biological basis for crime, such as genetic make-up. For example, Aaron Hernandez was prosecuted for murder in 2015. Following his death in 2017, it was discovered that he was suffering from a degenerative brain condition that made his behaviour more violent and aggressive, which may have led him to commit murder. **(2K)**

However, gender and mental health may be more likely to cause crime. Men are more likely to commit crimes of violence due to them having testosterone, which is linked to increased aggression. **(1K)** Also, studies of prisoners have shown that they are more likely to suffer mental illnesses such as personality disorders like schizophrenia. Over 80% of Scottish prisoners have at least one mental illness which could have caused them to commit crime. In addition, around 90% of prisoners are male, which shows a potential link to testosterone theory. **(2K)** Therefore, Lombroso's theory may not explain criminal behaviour, but gender and mental health is more closely linked to aggression, violence and increased criminality. **(1A)**

Durkheim tried to explain crime as being caused by a malfunction in society. According to Durkheim, society has a collective conscience, which means that most people have a revulsion towards crime, but sometimes this collective conscience is weakened by stress, crisis or frustration in society and people turn to crime as a reaction to this crisis. **(2K)** This can be seen in the London riots where the rules of society were broken and mass criminality in the form of looting and rioting took place. Society had malfunctioned and people reacted criminally to this malfunction. **(1A)**

8K 2A 0E 1S = 11/20

Marker's commentary

The candidate scores highly on knowledge with relevant discussion of some theories and gives some relevant examples. However, the response is very light on analysis and evaluation of how significant or important these causes are. A little more on the higher-order skills of analysis and evaluation would take this Grade C response up to a good B or even an A.

Grade A response

There are many causes of crime including biological, sociological and psychological. This essay will look at some of the key theories and thinkers.

One cause of crime is Lombroso's theory that crime is biological and caused by a person's physical features. Lombroso believed back in the 1880s that people with certain characteristics were more likely to be more criminally minded than others. He believed that having a distinctive athletic torso, large hands and a crooked nose were indicators of someone being likely to be a criminal. He based his studies on Italian prisoners who he believed had similar characteristics. **(2K)** Nowadays, his theories are widely discounted as not very scientific and not really correct.

Others believe that a person's sex plays a more influential role in whether someone is likely to commit certain crimes. It is believed that males are more likely to commit certain crimes, usually of a violent or sexual nature, than women. **(1K)** For example, 90% of all murders committed in Scotland were by men, with men accounting for 85% of all crime. **(1K)** This highlights the influence that a person's sex has on crime. This may be due to a man's biological make-up, such as genes or too much testosterone. Or, it might be that men are socially conditioned to be more aggressive and violent. **(1A)**

Another theory behind the causes of crime is that of Emile Durkheim. He believed that the basis of crime is rooted in society and that crime has a necessary function to play in society as it can indicate that society is not functioning as it should. **(1K)** For example, the London riots of 2011 indicated that the discrimination against young black men in London by police carrying out stop and search and Operation Trident was leading to growing anger and tension between these two groups and that something had to be done to resolve this. **(1K)** According to Durkheim, this showed that crime is necessary to pinpoint where society is failing some of its people. **(1A)**

However, it is argued that Strain Theory is more influential. This is the belief that the desire to compete and keep up in a capitalist society puts strain on individuals and some resort to crime to achieve those things unobtainable through normal hard work. **(1A)** Again, the London riots show that many people stole expensive training shoes and TVs during the riots, which backs up Strain Theory. **(1A)**

The Chicago School theory also helps explain crime, with the emphasis on those that are poor being more likely to commit crime due to their standing in society and desire to survive. **(1K)** Being poor can lead to some people committing crime, and this is a strong influence on them committing crime. That said, rich people also commit crime, with white collar crime such as fraud and insider dealing being committed by the very well-off. **(1K)**

Mental health can also cause crime. Someone with schizophrenia or severe multiple mental disorders can commit crime as their judgement function and ability to take rational decisions can be impaired. **(1K)** Also, knowing the difference between good and bad can be impaired too. For example, 30% of young offenders suffer ADHD and 80% of adult Scottish prisoners had some form of mental illness. **(1K)** This shows that mental illness can be a factor in influencing someone's level of criminality. **(1E)**

Therefore, there are many theories of crime, with some being based on a person's biology and others basing it on the role of society and levels of poverty. **(1E)**

8K (capped at 8) 4A 2E 2S = 16/20

Marker's commentary

A thorough response in terms of the areas covered. The candidate has a good balance of knowledge, examples, analysis as well as evaluation. A bit more evaluation would have boosted this grade up to a high A.

---

5 'Crime can impact on many different groups.' Discuss.

Grade C response

Crime can have an economic impact on victims. They can lose money as they may have to spend money on alarms and CCTV. Victims may also have to take time off work to recover from the crime and this may make them poorer financially. **(1K)** It may also cost more in insurance premiums. For example, after a crime 73% of people lose between £100 and £1000 due to being a victim of crime. **(1K)** Victims may also lose confidence in themselves, particularly if they are a victim of assault or crimes of violence. **(1K)** They can suffer PTSD and depression as well as anxiety and stress. They often find it hard to reconnect with friends or family and view the world differently. **(1K)** This shows that victims are affected by a loss of confidence and they find it hard to deal with other people and wider society.

Families of victims also suffer due to crime as it can affect the relationship they have with the victim and it could lead to a breakdown of their relationships, particularly in crimes such as sexual assault and rape. **(1A)** Victims can often be distant and need counselling, which can put a strain on their marriage and could lead to a break-up. **(1K)** Victims' families may also suffer financially, particularly if the victim has to take an extended period of time off to recover from the trauma and psychological damage that the crime has caused. **(1K)**

Criminals can also suffer due to their crimes, especially if they are sent to prison. They could lose their house and it could lead to family break-up due to the time being spent apart from their loved ones, which can cause additional stress to them and their families. **(1K)** Their families also find it hard to deal with the consequences of their criminality and may feel a sense of shame about a member of their family being a criminal. **(1K)**

8K 1A 0E 1S = 10/20

Marker's commentary

The candidate describes very well the issue of crime impacting on individuals, but struggles to give analysis and evaluation to build upon their knowledge marks. They should discuss the potential impact of crime and its consequences on the victim. Using words and link phrases such as 'this highlights …' and 'this shows …' followed by an analytical point would add to and boost this candidate's marks.

Grade A response

Crime can have an impact on many different groups, such as the victims, the criminals themselves and the families of both groups. This essay will look at the impact of crime on these groups.

Crime can have a significant impact on the victim due to loss of income. When someone becomes a victim of crime, such as theft or burglary, this could lead to a loss of income as the victim may have to spend extra income to replace the stolen items or repair the damage to property, or even buy security alarms in order to feel safer in their own homes. **(2K)** This could mean that the victim will suffer financially for a time after the crime. This can impact on the victim if they are struggling financially, particularly as housebreaking is more likely to occur in poorer areas where the victim may not have insurance. **(1A)**

Crime can also affect the victim psychologically, as experiencing crime can lead to trauma which may take some time to recover from. This can lead to depression, anxiety, extra stress and even PTSD, which could also affect their relationships with other people close to them and potentially affect their mental health over the long term. **(1K)** Being a victim of crime can make people scared about going outside and can lead to an impact on their social and working life. Therefore, crime can have a huge psychological impact on their well-being and mental health. **(1A 1E)**

Therefore, crime has a financial and psychological impact on the victim which can lead to financial difficulty and further psychological stress.

Another group which crime can impact upon is the criminals themselves. They can find it very difficult to get a job if they have a criminal record or have spent time in prison. This impacts financially on them and they may suffer unemployment and increased poverty which may in turn lead them to commit further crime. **(1K 1A)** In 2017, 27% of criminals who left prison found work, with around three-quarters of former prisoners struggling and suffering unemployment. Also, by being sent to prison, they may lose their house and will certainly lose any employment that they had. **(1K)** This can also lead to the break-up of criminals' relationships and marriages, which could cause increased stress, anger and depression, which could lead to further criminality on their behalf. Therefore, incarceration can significantly affect a criminal, not only while in prison but also after they leave due to increased risk of unemployment, poverty and deprivation. They could end up homeless and may suffer mental health problems. **(1A 1E)**

Another group likely to be impacted by crime is the families of criminals. If someone has committed a crime, people may label the family and stigmatise them, which could lead to them being shunned at school or in the community. **(1K)** This can impact on them socially and psychologically due to increased isolation, which could lead to them leaving or losing their home. They are also more likely to end up in poverty and with increased deprivation if a member of their family, particularly the father, is sent to prison. **(1A)**

Therefore, we can see that crime can have a huge impact on the victim and their families, but also the criminal and their family too. This impact can be social, financial and also psychological. **(1E)**

6K 5A 3E 2S = 16/20

Marker's commentary

This candidate covers some creditworthy areas and describes some of the impacts on the individual caused by crime. The strength of this response comes from the really good use of analysis and evaluation, which scores 8 marks in total. Good use of phrases such as 'This can impact …' and 'This can lead …' are really good stems for analysis and evaluation.

International issues: World issues

6   'Some factors are more important than others in causing the world issue you have studied.' Discuss.

Grade C response

One cause of terrorism is religion. Islamic extremists believe that terrorism is an acceptable way to force or impose their religious views on others. An example of this is ISIS, who follow an extreme interpretation of Islam which is anti-western and promotes sectarian violence against other Islamic groups in order to impose Sharia Law. **(2K)** They have been responsible for terrorist attacks across the Middle East as well as attacks in London, Paris, New York, Berlin, etc. This shows that religious extremism can be a cause of terrorism. **(1A 1K)**

Another cause of terrorism can be political issues. Countries run by dictators are often oppressive and deny basic human and political rights to their people, such as the freedom to protest or fair elections. **(1K)** They often turn to terrorism in order for their voice to be heard or views to be considered. This is often linked to political nationalism as people want to have a say in how their country or region is organised, and they often want to be independent and run their region or country themselves. **(1K 1A)** For example, the Kurds in northern Turkey are fighting for their own homeland to be separate from Turkey and have resorted to terrorism and violence to try to force Turkey to grant them independence or recognise their demands. **(1K)**

Therefore, we can see that terrorism can be caused by religious, political and nationalist factors, with some of them linked to each other. **(1E)**

6K 1A 1E = 8/20

Marker's commentary

Firstly, this candidate does not cover enough areas for a B or an A grade. They need at least two or possibly three more points that are structured showing relevant knowledge, exemplification and analysis. They don't do this consistently enough. They do attempt to link political nationalism and terrorism, and they do give a really good example, but this response needs to focus on development and greater coverage.

Grade A response

Terrorism is the unlawful use of violence and intimidation, especially against civilians, in order to achieve a political aim. The threat of terrorism is a major national security risk for many countries, and it is not unique to the twenty-first century. Terrorism is highly concentrated geographically, but it is also a globally distributed phenomenon. There are many factors which cause terrorism, and these include: economic factors, social factors, political factors and religious factors.

It could be argued that political motivations are critically important factors that give rise to international terrorism. Terror groups can be motivated by nationalist separatist feelings, historical arguments or a feeling of opposition and under-representation within their government. In autocratic societies, military occupied areas, or even in the international arena where political expression is limited, groups opposing the current state of affairs may engage in terrorism as a principal method of extremism. **(1K)** In the case of national separatist movements such as the Basque separatist group, ETA, and pro-Palestinian terrorist group, Hamas, terrorists often take the unfairness of their treatment by governments that deprive them of identity, dignity, security and freedom as the main reason for joining terrorist groups. **(1K)** Reports on Palestinian suicide bombers systematically refer to historical grievances, such as resentment, humiliation, sorrow and the aspiration of vengeance and retaliations. It could be argued that Irish nationalist militant group, the IRA, are motivated by political factors relating to their desire to leave the UK and become part of the Republic of Ireland. The IRA have conducted bombing campaigns in Northern Ireland and England with the goal of causing economic harms and/or disruption. One example was in 2014, when a PSNI (Police Service of Northern Ireland) Land Rover was hit by a mortar bomb on Falls Road, Belfast. **(2K)** It could be stated that terrorism is often seen as a logical extension of the failure of politics. When people seek redress for their grievances through government, but fail to win their government's attention to their plight, they may resort to violence. The IRA and Hamas are cases in point. **(1A)**

There have been many links between poverty and terrorism. In view of the 70% adult unemployment rate in Gaza, it is easy to allude to the possibility that relative deprivation has helped trigger Palestinian terrorism. **(1K)** For example, with a GDP of less than $1000 throughout the Palestinian Territories, the very limited economic opportunities due to the unsettled Israeli–Palestinian conflict, and also the cultural prominence of the male wage-earner role, relative economic deprivation manifests itself in poverty, income inequality, unemployment and also a lack of economic opportunities. **(1K)** Therefore, this makes it easier for terrorist organisations to recruit frustrated and impoverished followers. **(1A)**

Terrorist group Boko Haram regularly pays those who will join them, and provides payments for both widows and the children of its fighters. Therefore, this suggests that terrorism can offer some people a way out of poverty. **(1A)** This information can be supported by some intelligence reports which say that at around $400 a month, ISIS pays its fighters nearly double what other groups in the region pay. It is believed that ISIS had built itself a total wealth of over $2 billion; this is far beyond what any other terrorist group has managed to gain in the past. **(1K)** ISIS also allows locals to dig at ancient sites, as long as those people give ISIS a percentage of the monetary value of anything that they find. Some researchers suggest that there is a direct correlation between poverty and the attraction of membership or support of terror groups. It can be suggested that acts of terrorism can be used for sheer financial gain. After Palestinian bombers commit suicide, their families earn subsequent social status, and are usually secured a financial reward. **(1A)**

Globalisation may create a sense of frustration, increasing tension and hostilities. This allows terrorist organisations to gain attention and entry to societies that have felt wronged by these perceived social injustices. Disputes over territory can cause individuals and groups to commit acts of terror – for example, the Palestinian Territories. **(1K)**

There is significant evidence which suggests that there is a strong link between social and economic issues and terrorism. Terrorism manifests itself in poverty, income inequality, unemployment and a lack of economic opportunities. In Iraq, the poverty–extremism connection took shape when materially deprived Sunni tribes in Anbar province allied with the force they had been paid to hold back (ISIS) as soon as the central government's much-needed financial compensation discontinued. **(1K)** This issue was also similar in Jordan, where support for ISIS has thrived in neglected, impoverished rural cities like Ma'an, where unemployment tops 25%. This suggests that people who turn to terrorism could have financial problems, and they may find that this is their only option to get out of this financial state. **(1A)**

It could be argued that economic reasons as a factor are significant to the rise of international terrorism. Terrorism manifests itself in poverty, income inequality, unemployment and a lack of economic opportunities. Economic deprivation, in turn, makes it easier for terrorist organisations to recruit frustrated followers. Some researchers suggest that there is a direct correlation between poverty and the attraction of membership or support of terror groups. **(2K 1A)**

In conclusion, there is not one clear factor which causes terrorist acts. Something which motivates one individual or group might not motivate another. For some groups, religion is a huge factor. For other groups, it might be a reaction to not having their voice heard or simply being poor, and others may have ideological reasons. For some, terrorists joining a group like ISIS may give them a sense of belonging, a purpose in life. It may also provide their family with much-needed money, as many can come from poorer areas. There is more than one factor overall as religion may be important in one place, but not in another. **(2E)**

8K (capped at 8) 6A 2E 2S = 18/20

Marker's commentary

The candidate is clearly knowledgeable about the issue. Indeed, they give too much knowledge and overshoot the maximum of 8 for knowledge. Even though they made 11 knowledge points, the most marks they will get will be 8 as that is the maximum. Try not to spend too much time and effort on marks that will be capped. That time could have been spent analysing or evaluating, and thus increasing the marks. There is possibly far too much in this response in terms of knowledge and a real danger that the candidate may run over time. The candidate should stick to the essay timings, which means they are not losing out on time when attempting the other questions.

---

7 To what extent have international organisations been effective at tackling terrorism?

Grade C response

Terrorism is growing around the world and many organisations have attempted to reduce the number of terrorist attacks. The UN, NATO, the EU and the African Union have all attempted to tackle terrorism.

One way the EU has tried to tackle terrorism is through the use of biometric passports, fingerprints and iris scanners. This makes it easier to know who exactly is travelling into Europe. **(1K)** They have also introduced checks on money transactions across Europe as well as the sharing of suspects' information between members. **(1K)** Also, the introduction of the European Arrest Warrant has made it easier to transfer suspects across borders and arrest those suspected of terrorist acts. **(1K)** However, some criticise the EU's actions as being too little too late as there have been attacks across Europe and they have not been able to stop them. They also criticise the EU for underfunding their counter-terrorist strategies. **(1A)**

The UN is another organisation that attempts to tackle terrorism by having a counter-terrorism strategy, as well as peacekeepers and the threat of military action in places such as the Middle East. **(1K)** NATO has a new role in fighting terrorism around the world. Alongside the US campaign in Afghanistan, NATO has been leading the International Security Assistance Force (ISAF) that is tasked with assisting the government of Afghanistan in creating a stable nation. **(1K)** They share information and train people in the Middle East to fight groups such as ISIS and Al-Qaeda. **(1K)** They have had some success in fighting ISIS in Syria and capturing terrorist suspects. **(1A)**

Overall, the EU have been the most successful at tackling terrorism. Although terrorism still exists, they have managed to break up European terrorist groups in Belgium and France as well as stopping potential attacks from happening. Despite this, some attacks still happen in Europe, so they are not fully effective. **(1E)**

6K 2A 1E 1S = 10/20

Marker's commentary

There is some detail in the opening paragraphs, but for a 20-mark response the candidate should consider covering more than just two organisations. They should cover three, or better still four, organisations and structure it with information about what those organisations have done with relevant examples to add value. They should then analyse how effective those organisations have been, showing success and failure, and finish with an overall evaluation of the points they have just made.

Grade A response

Terrorism is the unlawful use of violence and intimidation, especially against civilians, to achieve a political aim. The threat of terrorism is a major national security risk for many countries, and it is not unique to the twenty-first century. Terrorism is highly concentrated geographically, but it is also a globally distributed phenomenon. There are many reasons why international organisations are effective in tackling terrorism. Organisations include: the United Nations (UN), the European Union (EU), the North Atlantic Treaty Organization (NATO) and the African Union.

One international organisation I have studied which tackles terrorism is the UN. The UN have put peacekeepers in place to monitor the peace process in countries all over the world. **(1K)** UN peacekeepers, often known as 'Blue Berets', can include soldiers, police officers and civilian personnel. Military observers have remained in the Middle East to monitor ceasefires and to prevent isolated incidents from escalating, etc. to fulfil the regions' respective mandates. **(1K)** This shows that the UN have been effective in tackling terrorism, because if they were not, then they would not still be in the Middle East observing the peace of the countries. **(1E)**

However, the UN cannot act effectively against terrorism as they have failed in tackling terrorism as peacekeepers, because wars still continue, and the threat of terrorism still exists. **(1A)** The UN have more than 97,000 uniformed personnel coming from over 110 countries. It can be said that the strongest action that the UN can take is military action. In 2011, the UN passed a resolution which authorised air strikes against naval ships in Libya. **(1K)** This shows that the UN are effective in tackling terrorism as they assisted in the overthrow of Gaddafi, who helped arm terrorists such as the IRA, as well as for the Lockerbie Bombing. **(1A)** However, the UN is often described as a 'paper tiger' – it looks the part, acts the part, but is weak and often ineffective. Overall, although counter-terrorism intentions are of critical importance to peace and security throughout the world, it is fair to evaluate that because of the political self-interest of individual countries, there is often no cohesive approach to counter-terrorism strategies. **(1E)**

Another international organisation which I have studied is the EU. EU member states are committed to jointly fighting terrorism, making Europe safer for its citizens. Terrorism threatens our security, the values of our democratic societies, and the rights and freedoms of European citizens. Fighting terrorism is a top priority for the EU and its member states, as well as its international partners. **(2K)** The EU were effective in 2006 when they introduced a law known as the Data Retention Directive. This allows governments to hold on to all telephone records for one year, and this makes it possible to trace calls by terrorist suspects, therefore making this strategy of the EU effective. The EU have issued a directive on the prevention of the use of the financial system for the purpose of money laundering and the funding of terrorist acts. This directive tries to stop crime by making banks investigate and report any transactions which are more than €15,000. **(2K)** The EU have been effective in tackling terrorism as they are being extremely serious about the issue, and over 1000 suspects were arrested in 2016. However, it can be said that the EU have not been effective in tackling terrorism as terrorist attacks continue in many EU countries, and the number has gone up – for example, Paris, Barcelona and London. Overall, it can be said that the EU have had some success in tackling terrorism, but they have also had some failures. **(1A 1E)**

Another international organisation I have studied is NATO. NATO is a military alliance which was created following the end of the Second World War. Following the events on 11 September 2001, NATO invoked Article 5. This Article states that an attack on one member country is an attack on all. **(1K)** This is an important part of the measures which are taken to strengthen the Alliance's fight against terrorism. Under Operation Active Endeavour, NATO have ships which monitor shipping in the Mediterranean Sea and try to deter, defend, disrupt and protect against any terrorist attacks. **(1K)** By controlling ships in this area, it helps to secure one of the busiest trade routes in the world. Since the beginning of this strategy, NATO have stopped over 115,000 vessels. Since the 9/11 attacks, NATO increased their information sharing and, more importantly, intelligence sharing. **(1K)** This is done between member and non-member countries. This has been effective in tackling terrorism as analytical approaches to terrorism and its link to other transactional threats have been enhanced. **(1A)** Overall, NATO have been effective in tackling the issue of terrorism as there have been a greater number of successes in comparison to the number of failures. However, it can be argued that the UN are better at dealing with the threat of terrorism. **(1E)**

Overall, these organisations have had some success in tackling terrorism, particularly NATO and the EU in areas such as sharing of intelligence about suspects and protecting their members; however, they have not been fully successful as terrorist attacks still occur quite regularly in countries that are NATO and EU members, as terrorism is really difficult to spot, prevent and stop. **(2E)**

8K (capped at 8) 4A 6E 2S = 20/20

Marker's commentary

A well-structured and highly detailed response that deals in great detail with the actions and effectiveness of three organisations. A great answer.

International issues: World power

8   To what extent has the world power you have studied been effective in tackling social inequalities?

Grade C response

One policy is No Child Left Behind, which is aimed at improving the basic skills of all US schoolchildren. The federal Government have increased the spending on education. Reading and maths scores have increased and the gap between black and Hispanic children compared to white schoolchildren has narrowed. **(2K)** However, the levels are still very low compared to other developed countries. This policy has also been criticised because states make up their own tests and some states dumb down the tests to make them easier for kids in order to show that there has been an improvement. **(1K 1A)** National tests would ensure consistency, but that currently does not happen and shows that this policy may not be working fully. **(1E)**

Medicaid and Medicare are also policies that have been introduced to help the elderly and the poor with health issues. It ensures that these groups have basic healthcare if they fall ill. The funding for this has been cut, which means that many people are no longer covered by this policy. **(1K 1A)**

A final scheme to tackle inequalities is the Fiscal Stimulus that was introduced by Obama after the last world recession. This built schools, hospitals and roads and pumped billions of dollars into the economy, which led to jobs being created and money being spent in the economy. **(2K)** This helped the USA and led to many millions of Americans having jobs.

6K 2A 1E 1S = 10/20

Marker's commentary

The candidate needs to expand their knowledge base and discuss more than only two policies. The description and knowledge could also be improved upon by giving some examples and statistics of those affected by these policies. Analysis and evaluation is a bit weak and needs proper development.

Grade A response

Social inequalities still exist in the USA, with some groups more likely to suffer inequalities than others, particularly black people and Hispanics. **(1K)** The US Government have introduced some policies to try to tackle these inequalities at both federal and state-wide levels.

The Patient Protection and Affordable Care Act 2010 (Obamacare) was introduced to increase the quality and affordability of healthcare. There are currently around 45 million Americans without health insurance, many of them black and Hispanic Americans. **(1K)** Since its introduction, over 7 million Americans have benefited through Obamacare and have used the system. This is more than was expected. **(1K)** It is hoped that it will lead to all Americans having some form of health cover. **(1A)** However, since Trump was elected, many Republicans have criticised Obamacare as being socialised medicine and have called it unconstitutional. Trump is looking to reverse Obamacare and remove it, despite it benefiting those who access it. **(1A)** This shows that this policy, while having some success, may be removed and could lead to many minorities not having or being covered by health insurance. **(1E)**

The main policy to reduce child poverty in the USA is called Temporary Assistance for Needy Families (TANF). This programme is financed at a federal level, but is state run and is aimed at getting many single parents back into work. TANF is only available for a maximum of five years per recipient. **(1K)** Since it was introduced the child poverty rate has fallen, and shows that TANF has been a success. **(1A)** However, recently the eligibility rules for TANF have got stricter, which means that fewer people receive it. Some argue that the fall in child poverty is not due to TANF, and that instead it is due to an overall improvement in the economy and that the level of USA child poverty is still among the highest in the developed world, showing that despite improvements, the USA still lags behind other countries in terms of child poverty figures. **(1K 1A 1E)**

A final policy is No Child Left Behind, which is aimed at improving the basic skills of all US schoolchildren. The federal Government have increased the spending on education. Reading and maths scores have increased and the gap between black and Hispanic children compared to white schoolchildren has narrowed. **(2K)** However, the levels are still very low compared to other developed countries. This policy has also been criticised because states make up their own tests and some states dumb down the tests to make them easier for kids in order to show that there has been an improvement. **(1K 1A)** National tests would ensure consistency, but that currently does not happen and shows that this policy may not be working fully. **(1E)**

8K 5A 3E 2S = 18/20

Marker's commentary

This shows a great understanding and knowledge of individual policies and their effectiveness and success. It has really strong knowledge, analysis and evaluation. A strong response.

Test your knowledge and understanding: 'Evaluate' questions

Social issues in the United Kingdom: Social inequality

9   Evaluate the causes of health inequalities.

Grade C response

Smoking is a major cause of poor health, with many people dying young due to smoking. It can cause bronchitis, asthma as well as heart attacks, strokes and cancers such as lung and throat. Poorer people are more likely to smoke than those who are better off. For example, 35% of adults in deprived areas of Scotland were smokers compared to only 10% in the well-off and more affluent areas. **(2K)** Women are more likely to smoke than men. While the number of men dying of lung cancer has decreased over the last 30 years, the number of women with lung cancer has almost doubled. **(2K)** Excessive alcohol consumption can also lead to many health issues. People in Scotland suffer more health issues linked to alcohol than any other area in the UK. In Scotland, alcohol consumption is 25% higher than in England. **(1K)** This shows a link between lifestyle, geography and gender. Poverty also plays a part, with poorer people making worse lifestyle choices. **(1E)**

5K 1E = 6/12

Marker's commentary

The candidate hasn't covered enough ground to merit beyond a C grade. They need to give at least one, and probably two, more developed points with knowledge, examples and an attempt at analysis/evaluation to take this up to a B or even an A.

Grade A response

One cause of health inequality is poverty. There is a clear link between a person's wealth and their health. A poorer person is more likely to have poorer health and die younger than someone who is well off. **(1K)** In Glasgow, there can be a difference of over ten years in the life expectancy of someone in a poor area such as Shettleston or Townhead compared to someone in a more affluent area such as Giffnock or Newton Mearns. **(1K)** Much of this is down to living conditions, environmental factors and poor lifestyle choices. **(1E)**

Many reports have confirmed the link between poverty and poor health. The first report to confirm this link was the Black Report in 1980. Since then, many other reports and studies, such as the World Health Organization (WHO) Report and the National Records report, continue to confirm this link. **(2K)**

Professor Harry Burns discusses the biology of poverty to explain the very poor health statistics in Scotland. He argues that the collapse of heavy industry, generations of male unemployment and the collapse of community has created a generational cycle of poverty and poor health in the west of Scotland.

This highlights the clear link between poverty and poor health. **(2K)**

Location is linked to poverty and this in turn is clearly linked to poor health outcomes. Areas that have experienced severe deprivation are usually in urban parts of the UK. As an example, Glasgow has the ten most deprived areas in Britain. **(2K)**

These are the areas which suffer most from health inequalities, with high levels of morbidity and low life expectancy. They also have high levels of benefit dependency, showing that many of these factors are linked. **(1A)**

8K 2E = 10/12

Marker's commentary

Some good use of research and reports in this response. Clearly a knowledgeable candidate who makes good creditworthy links between factors. The only thing the candidate needs to do is ensure that they are using the information and knowledge shown to make valid evaluative comments – this would ensure an additional 1 or 2 marks.

Social issues in the United Kingdom: Crime and the law

10 Evaluate the social and economic impact of crime.

Grade C response

Crime has had a very high social cost that is often paid for by the victim or those living in areas of high crime. Many victims of crime will change their routine or not go out to areas of high crime. They will often move out of an area or their house if they have been a victim of violent or property crime. **(1K)** Many people will leave an area due to feeling that their own private space, such as their home, has been violated due to theft, robbery or burglary. **(1K)** People in areas of high crime are less likely to go out or socialise due to the fear of being a victim or their house being broken into. **(1K)** This will have an economic cost as they will need to pay higher insurance premiums for house or car insurance or they may not be able to afford home contents insurance, and they will not be insured, which means if they get broken into, they will lose everything and probably will not have the money to replace the things stolen. **(1K 1E)**

Finally, it costs the UK taxpayer around £6 billion per year in terms of policing, the courts and prison costs. This has to be paid through higher tax or money being taken from one budget in order to pay for police costs and the costs of trials. **(1K)** This highlights the economic cost of crime that is often paid for through higher taxes by ordinary hard-working individuals. **(1E)**

5K 2E = 7/12

Marker's commentary

A lazy and light response. The candidate needs to make more points and evaluate much more than they currently have. The more you write, the easier it is to move up the grades.

Grade A response

One social impact of crime is that it can impact on a specific area, particularly where there are high levels of crime. This can often lead to a cycle of deprivation and crime that means that people will move out of an area because of high crime rates and others will not want to move there. **(1K)** This can have an effect on property prices in the area and the area can become run down and a magnet for other types of crime. **(1K)** High levels of crime may damage the community spirit and result in less neighbourliness as people may simply want to keep themselves to themselves. **(1E)** High crime levels can also result in or contribute to environmental poverty such as increased vandalism and graffiti. Once an area is labelled a bad area it may become a ghetto where crime is very common to that location. **(1K)** James Wilson created a theory called 'Broken Windows Theory' which helps explain how an area can become run down and ghettoised due to rising levels of crime that is not tackled effectively by the police. **(1E)**

The social impact of crime on an area can have devastating consequences, particularly in the most deprived locations. In these areas people are 2.5 times more likely to be mugged or burgled than the national average, with people staying in social or council housing twice as likely to be victims of crime as those in private or bought houses. **(1K)** This can affect those living in these types of areas as they are more likely to be worried about being a victim of crime, and this may impact on their social life in terms of where they go and their normal everyday routine. **(1K)** This shows that crime can have a large social impact on those in poorer areas and the type of life they lead due to the fear of crime. **(1E)**

People on low incomes are over 1.5 times more likely to be a victim of mugging or burglary and four times more likely to feel very unsafe when walking home alone at night than those with higher incomes. **(1K)** The better-off can also afford to install home security measures such as CCTV and alarms. They can also afford to live in safer, lower crime areas than those who are poorer and are more likely to have home insurance. **(1K)** This shows that the poor are the hardest hit and least likely to cope socially or financially with being a victim of crime. **(1E)**

7K 4E = 11/12

Marker's commentary

A good, well-structured response. The candidate exhibits a good level of knowledge regarding the question and evaluates the point made very well. One more creditworthy and valid point or example made would have taken this up to full marks.

International issues: World power

11 Evaluate the impact that inequality has on a specific group that you have studied.

Grade C response

One group that I have studied that suffer inequality in the USA are black Americans. When it comes to healthcare, black Americans are likely to suffer more morbidity and mortality than white people. This means they are likely to have more illness and die younger than white people. Infant mortality is twice as high for black children compared to white children, and black mothers are five times more likely to die during childbirth than white mothers. **(1K 1E)** Also, black women have the highest death rates from heart disease, breast and lung cancer than any other ethnic group in the USA. This highlights the extreme inequality that exists in the USA among ethnic groups, with the issue of healthcare for black people suffering the worst healthcare outcomes. **(1K 1E)**

Also, black people are more likely than any other group to be arrested for violent crimes such as murder; 36% of those arrested for murder were black despite black people only making up 14% of the population. They are also more likely to be the victims of murder, with 47% of all murder victims being black, and black people account for around 39% of those arrested despite making up 14% of the population. **(2K)**

4K 2E = 6/12

Marker's commentary

The candidate needs to cover more areas in their answer. Some relevant points are made, but there need to be at least one or two more points to score higher. Making these additional points and giving examples to back them up, followed by evaluation or analysis would gain more marks.

Grade A response

The group I have studied are ethnic minorities in the USA. This includes black people, Hispanics and Asian Americans. Black people and Hispanics are likely to suffer more inequality in areas such as employment, education and housing than any other group in the USA.

In education, black people and Hispanics are more likely to drop out of school early and achieve poorer grades than any other group. **(1K)** This has an impact on their employment chances as well as wage levels and access to higher education, such as attending college or university. Around 25% of Hispanics and around 20% of black people drop out of school in the USA. **(1K)** This highlights that inequality exists in relation to education in the USA. In terms of educational achievement, black people and Hispanics do worse than any other group, with only 15% of Hispanics and 18% of black people graduating college compared to 35% of white people and 50% of Asian Americans. **(1K)** Again, this highlights the level of educational inequality in the USA. **(1E)**

In terms of housing, inequality also exists as black people and Hispanics are much less likely to own their own homes and are more likely to stay in run-down areas, known as projects, which tend to be poorer-quality housing and have levels of crime and other social problems such as drugs. **(1K)** For example, 80% of white people own their own homes compared to 40% and 45% of black people and Hispanics. **(1K)** Many black people struggle to get a mortgage because they are more likely to be unemployed or suffer extended periods of unemployment throughout their lives, with them often renting in run-down inner city areas. **(1K)** This highlights that social inequality exists for some groups more than others in the USA. **(1E)**

A final way that inequality exists among groups can be found by looking at the area of crime and justice. Despite being a minority of the population, black people and Hispanics make up the majority of the prison population across the USA; 40% of prisoners are black and a further 20% are Hispanic. **(1K)** For white Americans the rate of prison population is around 409 per 100,000 of the population compared with 1038 per 100,000 Hispanics and 4618 per 100,000 black Americans. **(1K)** Many explain this as being due to the fact that the American justice system discriminates against black people, especially when it comes to prison sentences. Black and Hispanic Americans are more likely to be jailed and receive longer sentences than white people for the same types of crimes. This highlights the extent of inequality in relation to crime and justice in the USA. **(2E)**

8K 4E = 12/12

Marker's commentary

Lots of relevant statistics and comparisons between the statistics. Excellent evaluation too. A worthy full-mark response.

International issues: World issues

12 Evaluate the impact of the world issue you have studied on governments.

Grade C response

Terrorism can affect governments in many ways. If a government are not seen to be acting tough with terrorists, it can cost them votes and they may lose elections. **(1K)** Many politicians have to be seen to be tough on terrorism as they don't want the government to appear weak. Following the New Zealand mosque shooting, the New Zealand Prime Minister immediately banned guns and took control of the situation. **(1K)** The public liked her firm response and she and her Government saw their popularity rise due to the action that they took following the attack. **(1E)** This shows that responding quickly and effectively can impact positively on a government. Failing to act or being seen to be slow can lead to a government being unpopular and could cost them political power. **(1E)**

Another impact on governments caused by terrorism could be social unrest. This was seen in Germany after they took in around 1 million Syrian refugees. **(1K)** There have been attacks on refugee hostels as well as growing numbers of right-wing anti-immigrant marches that have been met by anti-fascist demonstrations against them which has led to confrontations and riots. **(1E)**

3K 3E = 6/12

Marker's commentary

A fairly light response here. The candidate makes valid points and an attempt at evaluation, but there is not enough content to merit any more marks than they have been given. At least another paragraph, but probably two, with content that includes up-to-date knowledge of the impact of terrorism on specific countries (France, UK, USA, etc.) backed up with examples and some evaluation of the impact (more fear, expense of hunting terrorists or increased security) would achieve more marks and a higher grade for the candidate.

Grade A response

One impact of terrorism on a country could be an increased cost to the economy, caused by loss of tourism and trade, and growing unemployment. Following the Tunisian beach attack, many people cancelled their holidays there, which had a huge impact on the economy of the country. **(1K)** Hotels had to close and people lost their jobs. This had a knock-on effect on the economy as Tunisians employed in tourism were no longer working and were not spending money in the Tunisian economy. **(1E)** Tourism was also affected after the Paris attacks as many Scottish schools and councils pulled out of school trips to Paris, which saw a decrease in the amount of money that the French received. **(1K)** This shows that terrorism can affect tourism, which in turn can affect the economy of an area.

Terrorism can also affect governments due to the number of refugees created by terrorist attacks. In countries that border Syria, such as Jordan and Turkey, there was a huge influx of refugees, which affected the infrastructure of those countries as governments had to provide medicines, shelter, education and food for the refugees. **(1K)** This was costly and had a negative impact on these governments, which led to social problems and increased tensions. This shows that terrorism can impact negatively on governments through increased demand for services and costs of providing these. **(1E)**

It can also lead to greater political tensions and a greater chance that these countries may be targets for terrorist attacks themselves. For example, since the Syrian conflict, there has been a growing number of terrorist attacks in Turkey and Iraq. **(1K)** These countries are more unstable than they were in the past, due to terrorism in a neighbouring country. **(1E)** There have been attempts to overthrow the Turkish Government and political instability in Iraq and all across the region due to the instability caused by terrorist attacks and civil war in Syria. **(1K)**

This shows that terrorism can have an economic, social and political impact in countries, either directly or indirectly affected by terrorism. **(1E)**

5K 4E = 9/12

Marker's commentary

An A-grade response, but only just. The candidate needs to ensure that they are a safe A-grade pass. Developing some of the points made or even discussing the impact of terrorism on the UK (there is plenty to write about in relation to the impact of terrorism in the UK) would see them move up by a few more marks into safe A-grade territory.

Test your knowledge and understanding: 'Analysis' questions

Social issues in the United Kingdom: Social inequality

13 With reference to a group you have studied, analyse the impact of inequality on that group.

Grade C response

One inequality I have studied is gender inequality, with women suffering more inequality than men. Women are often paid significantly less than men for doing similar types of jobs. This is known as the gender pay gap, with women being paid around 15% less than men. **(1K)** They also tend to do poorer-paid part-time jobs, such as cooking, clerical work or childcare, with little chance of promotion or breaking through the 'glass ceiling' – only a very small percentage of women occupy the top jobs in major firms or industries, such as Parliament or in the FTSE 100 top UK companies. **(2K)**

Women often suffer discrimination in some jobs which are sometimes seen as being jobs for men, such as building, plumbing or electrician services. This puts many women off applying for these jobs. **(1K)** However, in some areas, such as medicine and nursing, there are more women than men, which shows that women are making positive progress in some areas more than men. **(1K)** Women still suffer discrimination with around 30,000 women each year losing their job because they are pregnant despite this being illegal. **(1K)**

6K 0A = 6/12

Marker's commentary

A short answer with two points covered and creditworthy knowledge, but the answer is let down by a lack of consistent analysis. Indeed, no analysis has been provided, which means that the candidate can only score a maximum of 8 marks.

Grade A response

Women across our society suffer from gender inequality in terms of jobs. As women are becoming more and more independent and likely to work full-time careers and part-time careers, they now play a crucial role in our economy. Women are more likely to work part time and in lower-paid jobs, and are generally paid less overall. **(1K)** This shows how inequality still exists even though more women are now working. **(1A)** Women are much more likely to work the '5Cs', which are jobs that are low paid, have flexible hours and are likely to be part time. These jobs are cashiering, catering, cleaning, caring and clerical careers. **(1K)** Women working these low-paid part-time jobs are paid 32% less than those working full time. In 2010, although the number of men and women working was almost the same, more women were working part time. **(1K)** Overall, as we can see more women work in part-time and low-paid jobs, gender inequality still needs improvement. **(1A)**

Although more women are working now than ever before, there is still gender inequality that exists among types of jobs and means of progression within those jobs. It has been shown that women find it very difficult to find employment in high positions. This is what is known as the 'glass ceiling' and means that women are stopped by what is almost like an invisible barrier. **(1K)** Although women have been proven to do better academically, men still occupy the top positions. As two-thirds of girls achieve five or more National 5 qualifications, and only 52% of boys do this, girls have been proven to excel further than boys. This can be seen again as 61% of all first-class degrees are achieved by women in the UK. As only 15% of senior police officers are women and a shocking 6% of top army officers are women, we can see how inequality within employment still exists. **(1K 1A)** It can also be said that women who are aged 20–35 are much less likely to be given promotion as they are likely to take maternity leave or get married, which would reduce their hours from full time to part time. **(1K)**

However, we can see some progress has been made in areas such as business and politics. For example, Karren Brady has become CEO of West Ham United, and figures such as Nicola Sturgeon, Theresa May and Ruth Davidson have become leaders of top political parties across British and Scottish politics. Although improvement has been made in some areas, there are still many aspects of our society that show gender inequality towards women still exists. **(1K 1A)**

Inequality for women also exists in terms of pay. As the 'pay gap' exists, this is a very large aspect of inequality and discrimination against women. For every pound that a man makes working part time, a woman will only earn 65p. And for every pound that a man earns working full time, a woman will only earn 83p. Over a lifetime, it has been calculated that women will earn around £300,000 less than men. It has also been said that it will be around 65 years until the full-time pay gap is closed and around 125 years until the part-time pay gap no longer exists. **(2K)**

As women earn much less, they are less likely to receive a full pension. This shows how much improvement is needed to eliminate this discrimination for women. **(1A)**

8K (capped at 8) 4A (capped at 4) = 12/12

Marker's commentary

An excellent response. A sophisticated and very knowledgeable response with consistent analysis throughout. Lots of areas covered with great use of statistics.

Social issues in the United Kingdom: Crime and the law

14 Analyse the effectiveness of custodial sentences.

Grade C response

Prison is one way that society can deal with convicted criminals. Currently there are over 90,000 prisoners jailed in UK prisons, with it costing around £40,000 per year to keep someone locked up. **(1K)** Many people think that this cost is just too high, particularly for those convicted of fairly minor offences such as housebreaking and petty theft. **(1A)** However, a majority of the UK public think that prison should be used and those that get caught committing criminal acts should be locked up and punished for their offences. **(1K)** Also, prison works as it protects members of the public from dangerous and violent criminals. This shows that despite the cost, prison is effective as it protects the public and punishes individuals for their criminal acts. **(1K)** However, prisons are often labelled as 'universities of crime', which means that prisoners sometimes leave with more knowledge of how to commit more and different crimes, as they share information and knowledge with other prisoners who they are locked up with. They may also get to know different drug dealers and therefore create more contacts and a wider network of dealers that they can use when they are released. **(2K)**

5K 1A = 6/12

Marker's commentary

A very light answer in terms of coverage. The candidate needs to add more knowledge and analysis to their answer. What they give is creditworthy and fairly relevant, but more knowledge and analysis is needed for them to go from a C pass to either a B or A pass.

Grade A response

Prison is one way that society can deal with convicted criminals. Currently there are over 90,000 prisoners jailed in UK prisons with it costing around £40,000 per year to keep someone locked up. **(1K)** Many people think that this cost is just too high, particularly for those convicted of fairly minor offences such as housebreaking and petty theft. **(1A)** However, a majority of the UK public think that prison should be used and those that get caught committing criminal acts should be locked up and punished for their offences. **(1K)** Also, prison works as it protects members of the public from dangerous and violent criminals. This shows that despite the cost, prison is effective as it protects the public and punishes individuals for their criminal acts. **(1K)**

One way that prison can be seen to be effective is that it acts as a deterrent for those who may be thinking of committing crime, but will think twice if others are given a heavy sentence for a similar crime. **(1K)**. This can be seen in the London riots of 2011. Many rioters were given very long sentences for fairly minor crimes in order to deter other rioters from committing these types of crimes or taking part in the riot. **(1K)** For example, someone was jailed for two years for stealing a pair of trainers. Many argued that this was to deter others from taking part in the riot and committing similar crimes. **(1K)**. Therefore, we can see that prison can often be used to deter others from committing similar crimes. **(1A)**

However, some people think that prison does not work, as many criminals often end up back in prison after a short space of time. Prison clearly does not deter criminals from committing crime nor is it effective at rehabilitating prisoners from continuing with a life of crime. Seventy-five per cent of short-term prisoners reoffend within two years of release. **(1K 1A)** Prison is often described as a 'revolving door' for this reason. **(1K)** Therefore, we can see that prison is not effective as it does not rehabilitate or deter prisoners from committing further crimes. **(1A)**

8K 4A = 12/12

Marker's commentary

An excellent response. Some very good knowledge is shown by the candidate in terms of crimes, and some good use of examples that add value to the response backed up with some very relevant and focused analysis. A good variety of points covered. An excellent answer.

International issues: World power

15 Analyse the powers of the executive branch of government.

Grade C response

The President of the USA is a very powerful individual with powers coming mainly from the US Constitution. However, the President is not all powerful and often many of the powers that they have are checked and balanced by the other branches of government – the Legislative and the Judicial branch. **(1K)**

One power that the President has is to suggest new policies. This often takes place during the State of the Union address every January, where the President will lay out what they would like to see Congress discuss, debate and introduce in the coming year. **(1K)** For example, Obama used the State of the Union address to suggest that Obamacare should be introduced. **(1K)** However, Congress does not need to discuss or debate this. It will often depend upon the political composition of the Congress. **(1A)** Democrat Presidents are more likely to see their proposals introduced if there is a Democrat Congress. A Republican Congress can simply block any legislation proposed by a Democrat President. **(1K)**

The President also has the power of Executive Order, which means that they can bypass Congress in terms of the introduction of a law if they feel that it is in the national interest to do so. **(1K)**

5K 1A = 6/12

Marker's commentary

The candidate makes a good attempt at covering knowledge of the power of the President but doesn't go far enough or in as much detail to score highly. They need to give at least one or two more points which are then analysed with regard to how powerful the President is and the checks and balances which exist limiting their power.

Grade A response

The President of the USA is a very powerful individual with powers coming mainly from the US Constitution. However, the President is not all powerful and often many of the powers that they have are checked and balanced by the other branches of government – the Legislative and the Judicial branch. **(1K)**

One power that the President has is to suggest new policies. This often takes place during the State of the Union address every January, where the President will lay out what they would like to see Congress discuss, debate and introduce in the coming year. **(1K)** For example, Obama used the State of the Union address to suggest that Obamacare should be introduced. **(1K)** However, Congress does not need to discuss or debate this. It will often depend upon the political composition of the Congress. **(1A)** Democrat Presidents are more likely to see their proposals introduced if there is a Democrat Congress. A Republican Congress can simply block any legislation proposed by a Democrat President. **(1K)**

As Commander-in-Chief of the Armed Forces, the President can mobilise troops and invade other countries. However, they cannot declare war on another country. **(1K)** Only Congress has the power to do this by voting for it. Also, if the President sends troops to another country, the finance for that has to come from and be approved by Congress. **(1K)** If Congress don't agree with the President's actions, they can vote to cut back the finance and money available for that. This shows that despite having many powers, the President can be stopped by Congress from fully carrying out the President's powers. **(1A)**

The President has to ensure that all of their actions are constitutional. That is, they are within the rules as laid out by the Constitution. **(1K)** They cannot go beyond the powers laid out in it. If they do, the Supreme Court can declare the President's actions unconstitutional and it could mean that the President is removed from office and impeached. **(1A)** This again highlights some of the limits to the power of the President. They may have many powers but they are not all powerful. **(1A)**

7K 4A = 11/12

Marker's commentary

Some very good knowledge and understanding of the role and powers of the President here. There is also a good, solid understanding of the limits to Presidential power and strong analysis. The candidate needs one more knowledge point to guarantee full marks.

International issues: World issues

16 Analyse the impact that the world issue you have studied has had on individuals affected by the issue.

Grade C response

Terrorism is an international issue which has a major impact on individuals. Terrorism can have many impacts upon individuals within a society, such as increased poverty, homelessness, disease as well as a 'human cost'. Homelessness is a major issue affecting many people in Nigeria due to terrorist group Boko Haram causing much disruption in people's lives, homes and communities. **(1K)** As many as 100,000 people have been killed by the group, leaving many orphans and widows. It is also estimated that over 300 churches have been bombed by them, as well as over 150 schools. **(1K)** This has created fear and increased numbers of refugees, with thousands fleeing their homes and villages. Despite this, many are too poor to leave. Therefore, we can see that terrorism can have a devastating impact on individuals. **(1A)**

It has also caused increased unemployment as businesses have closed and many people are scared to go about their normal everyday lives, such as going to work or school. This has had an impact on people's incomes and poverty levels, with many individuals struggling to cope financially. **(1K)**

This can also cause mental health problems and feelings of depression and despair, with increased poverty, little money and the fear of being attacked. **(1K)**

Disease is another issue that affects individuals, particularly in developing countries affected by terrorism as many refugees are created, who live in overcrowded camps with poor sanitation that are breeding grounds for diseases. **(1K)**

Therefore, terrorism has a major impact on individuals in terms of poverty, death, increased fear, refugees and disease, particularly in poorer countries. **(1A)**

5K 2A = 7/12

Marker's commentary

The candidate scores for some knowledge of impacts and gives some statistics, but only makes slight reference to analysis. They should make more attempt at analysing the knowledge points they make.

Grade A response

Terrorism has been defined as the use of violence in order achieve a social, religious or political change in the actions of a government. The most effective weapon used by terrorists is perhaps not the act itself but the fear that the threat of a terrorist act instils, not just on those affected, but also on wider society. However, it can also impact on the lives of individuals.

One way that terrorism affects individuals is that it can cause poverty. Within Nigeria, which is one of the five countries most affected by terrorism alongside Iraq, Afghanistan, Syria and Pakistan, there are many millions of people unemployed. **(1K)** This is due to a decrease in jobs available, as many businesses will either not invest or close their businesses down due to terrorist attacks. This is a major issue in Nigeria as many businesses opened due to tourism. However, with many parts of the country now unsafe, tourism has declined. **(1A)** After the terrorist attacks in Tunisia and Egypt, tourism was seriously affected as many people cancelled holidays, which led to an increase in unemployment and poverty in those particular areas. This affects many young people in the area who would likely be employed in the tourist industry. **(1K)**

Those within the northern areas of Nigeria are 40% more likely to be in poverty than in the south. This is due to the fact that attacks by Boko Haram are more likely to take place there. Also, in Kano over 100,000 people have moved out of their homes due to terrorist attacks. This has made poverty levels soar, with many individuals affected by terrorism. **(2K)**

Another way terrorism affects individuals is that it can increase the number of refugees and can cause an increase in poor health and diseases. With the increase in poverty and the rise of refugee camps, many are not able to access clean water or sanitation facilities, and this has caused the spread of diseases such as cholera and typhoid. **(1K)** The increased number of refugees has caused diseases to grow, as they are living in overcrowded camps with very limited access to toilets or medicines. Ten of the eleven countries with the highest number of refugees are affected by terrorism. **(1K)** This shows that terrorism can affect individuals as it causes a country to have thousands of refugees, which reduces access to facilities and can cause the spread of diseases. **(1A)**

Another impact of terrorism on individuals is that it can lead to psychological trauma and post-traumatic stress disorder and other psychological issues. Following the Manchester, London and Paris attacks, there was a sharp increase in the number of people seeking counselling and psychological help as a result of either witnessing the attacks or seeing them in the media. **(1K)**

Therefore, we can see that terrorism can affect individuals in terms of increased poverty, homelessness, violence and psychological issues, depending on where the terrorism occurs. Poverty tends to increase in developing countries affected by terrorism. **(1A)**

7K 3A = 10/12

Marker's commentary

The candidate covers some creditworthy areas and discusses the impact psychologically as well as the impact on health and poverty. There is some solid analysis to accompany the knowledge shown. One more point or some development of points made could have taken this response to full marks.

Paper 2
Objectivity questions

17 *You can be credited in a number of ways to a maximum of 10 marks.*

Evidence that supports the view (an outstanding victory for Donald Trump):

▸ Source A, all of the opinion polls predicted a Clinton victory, so Trump's victory was outstanding.

▸ Source A, Trump won four of the five key swing states.

▸ Source A, Trump won the clear support of the rich, the poorly educated white voters including women and those over the age of 64.

▸ Source B, non-college-educated white voters (67%) supported Trump.

▸ Source B, 53% of men voted for Trump compared to 41% for Clinton.

▸ Source B, 58% of white people voted for Trump compared to 37% for Clinton.

▸ Source A, Trump received 306 Electoral College votes compared with 232 for Clinton.

▸ Source C, a clear victory for Trump in terms of Electoral College votes – he won 56.8%.

Response 1

It was an outstanding victory for Trump as he won almost 60% of the white votes and won four of the five key swing states, such as Florida and Wisconsin.

(Total 2 marks: evidence linked from two sources)

Evidence that opposes the view (an outstanding victory for Donald Trump):

▸ Source A, Clinton actually won more votes than Trump – 65.5 million compared to 62.8 million for Trump.

▸ Source A, Clinton won 88% of the black vote and 71% of the Hispanic and Asian vote.

▸ Source A, unmarried women favoured Clinton by 62% to 33%.

▸ Source B, Clinton won the female vote – 54% to 42%.

▸ Source B, overwhelming support for Clinton among Hispanic voters – 74% to 21%.

▸ Source B, clear support for Clinton among those aged 18–44 – 52% to 40%.

▸ Source C, Clinton won 48.1% of the popular vote compared to only 46.2% for Trump.

▸ Source C, Trump won fewer popular votes than Romney did in the 2012 Presidential Election – he only won 46.2% compared to 47.1% for Romney.

Response 2

It was not an outstanding victory as Trump failed to win the popular vote. Clinton received 2 million more votes than Trump.

(Total 1 mark: one relevant piece of evidence from one source)

For full marks, you must make an overall judgement as to the extent of the accuracy of the given statement.

Examples of possible overall judgements:

Response 3

The statement is correct to a very limited extent. It is true that Trump had outstanding support from poorly educated white voters and had a clear victory in the Electoral College. However, he failed to win the popular vote and had far fewer votes than Clinton.

(Total 2 marks)

Response 4

The statement is partly correct as he clearly won the key swing states and the white vote.

(Total 1 mark)

Response 5

The statement is true to a certain extent.

(Total 0 marks)

Conclusion questions

18 *You can be credited in a number of ways to a maximum of 10 marks.*

Possible approaches to answering the question – the link between weight issues and income:

Response 1

There is a clear link between poverty and those who experience weight issues, including obesity. This is supported in Source A, which indicates the lowest social classes have the highest levels of obesity.

(Total 1 mark: a valid overall conclusion based on evidence from one source)

Response 2

There is a clear link between poverty and those children who experience weight issues, including obesity. This is supported in Source A, which shows that Scottish children from the poorest areas of Scotland are twice as likely to be obese compared to children from the wealthiest areas. This is further supported in Source B, which shows that among Primary 1 pupils there is a clear contrast between those living in areas of poverty compared to those in the least deprived or wealthiest areas – 12% of children in the most deprived areas are obese compared to 7% in the wealthiest areas.

(Total 3 marks: a valid overall conclusion based on complex synthesis between two sources)

Response 3

There is a clear link between poverty and those who experience weight issues, including obesity.

(Total 0 marks: conclusion with no supporting evidence)

Possible approaches to answering the question – the link between weight issues and gender:

Response 4

Women experience more weight issues than men. This is supported in Source A, which shows that women with limited educational qualifications suffer more from obesity than men.

(Total 1 mark: a valid overall conclusion based on evidence from one source)

Response 5

More women are overweight (including obese) than men. This is supported in Source B, which shows that in some of the age categories, the figures for women are significantly higher, for example in the age group 65–74 the figure for obesity and being overweight is 35% for women and 24% for men.

(Total 1 mark: a valid overall conclusion based on evidence from one source)

Possible approaches to answering the question – the link between drug-related deaths and income:

Response 6

There is a clear link between poverty and deaths from drug abuse.

(Total 0 marks: conclusion with no supporting evidence)

Response 7

The highest number of drug-related deaths are in the poorest areas of Scotland. Source 1 states that drug use and related deaths is 17 times higher in the poorest areas such as Glasgow and Dundee. This is further supported in source C which shows that Glasgow has double the number of drug-related deaths per 1000 of population (0.23), compared to wealthier areas such as Grampian (0.12). This highlights the extent of the crisis.

(Total 3 marks: valid overall conclusion based on detailed evidence from two sources with evaluative comment)

Possible overall conclusion about the trend in drug-related deaths in Scotland:

Response 8

The trend in drug-related deaths is that the numbers are increasing.

(Total 0 marks: overall conclusion without supporting evidence)

Response 9

The trend in drug-related deaths is that the numbers are massively increasing. This is supported in source B, which states that the number of drug-related deaths has increased from 244 in 1996 to over 1000 by 2018. This surely has become a national crisis.

(Total 2 marks: overall conclusion with supporting evidence and evaluative comment)

Reliability questions

19 *You can be credited in a number of ways to a maximum of 8 marks.*

Possible approaches to answering the question:

Source A

Response 1

Source A is not reliable.

(Total 0 marks: no evidence or explanation provided)

Response 2

Source A is not reliable as it is an interview with a terrorist and only gives one person's perspective of the issue.

(Total 1 mark: straightforward evidence provided)

Response 3

Source A is reliable and trustworthy to a certain extent. It has been published by a UK newspaper, *The Independent*, and although it will be biased, the journalist – in this case Shehab Khan, the author – should have followed journalistic ethics and standards when researching and writing this piece.

(Total 2 marks: detailed evidence provided)

Source B

Response 4

Source B is trustworthy as it is published by Ipsos MORI, a highly respected and professional polling organisation used by many media outlets. The sample of people questioned is representative, meaning it reflects the diversity of the population.

(Total 2 marks: detailed evidence provided)

Source C

Response 5

Although Source C is from a respected news organisation, Channel 4, which has high trust ratings among UK sources of news, this was published in 2009, which reduces the article's reliability as events will have changed since then and it will not contain the most up-to-date information. Therefore, Source C's reliability is questionable.

(Total 2 marks: detailed evidence provided)

Examples of an overall conclusion on the most reliable source:

Response 6

Source A is the most reliable source as it is the most up to date, having been published on 30 January 2016.

(Total 1 mark: overall conclusion supported by evidence from one source)

Response 7

Source B is the most reliable source as the survey was carried out in January 2016 and is more up to date than Source C, which was published in 2009. Source B is also likely to be more objective than Source A, which is from a newspaper, and likely to be biased.

(Total 2 marks: overall conclusion supported by detailed evidence from all sources)

For full marks, you must make an overall judgement on the most reliable source.

Paper 1

Duration: 1 hour and 45 minutes

Total marks: 52

SECTION 1 – DEMOCRACY IN SCOTLAND AND THE UNITED KINGDOM – 12 marks

Attempt **ONE** Question from 1(a) **OR** 1(b) **OR** 1(c)

SECTION 2 – SOCIAL ISSUES IN THE UNITED KINGDOM – 20 marks

Part A Social inequality

Part B Crime and the law

Attempt **ONE** Question from 2(a) **OR** 2(b) **OR** 2(c) **OR** 2(d)

SECTION 3 – INTERNATIONAL ISSUES – 20 marks

Part C World power

Part D World issues

Attempt **ONE** Question from 3(a) **OR** 3(b) **OR** 3(c) **OR** 3(d)

Read the questions carefully.

You must clearly identify the question number you are attempting.

Use **blue** or **black** ink.

Section 1: Democracy in Scotland and the United Kingdom

Total marks: 12 marks
Attempt **ONE** Question from 1(a) **OR** 1(b) **OR** 1(c)

Question 1

MARKS

(a) Analyse the ways in which pressure groups can influence government decision-making.

12

You should refer to Scotland **or** the United Kingdom **or** both in your answer.

OR

(b) Analyse the impact of the UK's decision to leave the EU.

12

You should refer to Scotland **or** the United Kingdom **or** both in your answer.

OR

(c) Evaluate the main factors that influence voting behaviour.

12

You should refer to Scotland **or** the United Kingdom **or** both in your answer.

Section 2: Social issues in the United Kingdom

Total marks: 20 marks
Attempt **ONE** Question from 2(a) **OR** 2(b) **OR** 2(c) **OR** 2(d)

Question 2

Part A: Social inequality

Answers may refer to Scotland **or** the United Kingdom **or** both.

MARKS

(a) To what extent have government policies been successful in reducing inequality on a group you have studied?   20

OR

(b) Health inequalities are caused by more than one factor.   20
Discuss.

OR

Part B: Crime and the law

Answers may refer to Scotland **or** the United Kingdom **or** both.

(c) To what extent is deprivation the most important cause of crime?   20

OR

(d) Community-based sentences are more effective than prison sentences.   20
Discuss.

Section 3: International issues

> **Total marks: 20 marks**
> Attempt **ONE** Question from 3(a) **OR** 3(b) **OR** 3(c) **OR** 3(d)

Question 3

MARKS

Part C: World power

With reference to a world power you have studied:

(a) To what extent does this country have a major international influence?
Discuss.

20

OR

(b) The political system of this country effectively allows democratic participation.
Discuss.

20

OR

Part D: World issues

With reference to a world issue you have studied:

(c) The consequences of this issue can have a devastating impact on those affected.
Discuss.

20

OR

(d) To what extent have international organisations been effective in resolving this
issue?

20

[END OF PAPER 1]

Paper 2

Duration: 1 hour and 15 minutes

Attempt **ALL** questions

Total marks: 28

Read the questions carefully.

You must clearly identify the question number you are attempting.

Use **blue** or **black** ink.

Total marks: 28
Attempt **ALL** questions

Question 1

Study Sources A, B and C then attempt the question that follows.

SOURCE A

A surprise outcome in the 2016 USA presidential election

All of the opinion polls predicted that Hillary Clinton, the Democrat candidate, would win the USA presidential election. However, to the shock of most Americans, Donald Trump, the Republican candidate, gained a clear victory in the Electoral College, winning 306 votes compared to Clinton's 232. This surprise result made his victory appear outstanding.

The President of the USA is not chosen directly by the US people. Instead, presidents are elected by 'electors' who are chosen by popular vote on a state-by-state basis.

These 'electors' then award their states' Electoral College votes to the candidate with the greatest support in their state. The two major political parties are the Democratic Party and the Republican Party. There are other political parties that participate in presidential elections, and in 2016 several other presidential candidates took part. In total these candidates gained about 5% of the votes.

The number of Electoral College votes in each state depends on the size of the state. For example, Florida, which has a large population (19.5 m), receives 29 Electoral College votes compared to the three received by Vermont, which has a small population (0.6 m). There are 538 Electoral College votes in total. However, the popular votes achieved in a state are not shared proportionally between the leading candidates. In the 2016 presidential election in Florida, Donald Trump won 49.1% of the popular vote compared to 47.8% for Hillary Clinton, yet Trump received all of the 29 Electoral College votes.

The key to victory in the Electoral College is to win as many 'swing states' as possible (many states are either solid Democrat or Republican, and swing states are those where either candidate could win). In the 2016 election, Hillary Clinton won only one of the five key swing states. It was a close result in several of these swing states – Trump's combined lead in Florida, Michigan, Pennsylvania and Wisconsin was only around 85,000 votes.

Yet Hillary Clinton won the most popular votes (the total number of votes each candidate received across the country). Clinton received 65.5 million votes compared to 62.8 million votes for Trump.

Clinton's support among non-white people was lower than Obama received in 2012. However, she still won 88% of the black vote and 71% of Hispanic and Asian votes. Trump's main support came from the rich, and from poorly educated white voters, including women and those aged over 64. The gender vote was complicated, with unmarried women favouring Clinton by 62% to 33% and white married women favouring Trump by 53% to 43%. The turnout was only 55.6% compared to 57.5% in 2012.

Results in selected swing states

State	% of votes		Electoral College votes	
	Trump	Clinton	Trump	Clinton
Florida	48.6	47.4	29	0
Michigan	47.3	47.0	16	0
Wisconsin	47.2	46.5	10	0
Pennsylvania	48.2	46.5	20	0

MARKS

SOURCE B

USA presidential results 2016 and 2012: Popular vote (%) and Electoral College (%)

Party and candidate	Popular vote 2016	Popular vote 2012
Democrat: Clinton	48.1	51.0
Republican: Trump	46.2	47.1
Electoral College	2016	2012
Democrat	43.2	61.7
Republican	56.8	47.1

Note: Obama was the Democrat candidate and Romney was the Republican candidate in the 2012 presidential elections.

SOURCE C

Voting by gender, income, ethnicity, age and education in 2016 presidential election (%)

	Trump	Clinton
Gender		
Male	53	41
Female	42	54
Income		
Earning less than $40,000	41	53
Earning more than $40,000	49	47
Ethnicity		
White non-Hispanic	58	37
Hispanic	21	74
African American	8	88
Age		
18–44	40	52
Over 45	53	44
Education		
Non-college-educated white	67	27
College-educated white	49	45

Attempt the following question, using only the information in Sources A, B and C.

What conclusions can be drawn about the result of the 2016 presidential election?
You must draw conclusions about:

► the link between the popular vote and the Electoral College vote in the 2016 election
► the influence of age and ethnicity on voting behaviour in the 2016 election
► the influence of gender and income on voting behaviour in the 2016 election.

You must also make an overall conclusion on the factor which most influenced the result of the USA presidential election.

10

Question 2

Study Sources A, B and C then attempt the question that follows.

SOURCE A

Zero-hours contracts allow employers to hire staff with no set working hours. This means employees work only when they are needed by their employer, often at short notice. Payment depends on hours worked. This benefits employers as it reduces their wage bill and can increase profits. However, it can lead to a high turnover of staff and can impact on productivity. This type of work contract is being increasingly used by employers. In 2016 the figure stood at an estimated 900,000 compared to 650,000 in 2013. This represents 3% of the UK workforce. Well-known companies such as McDonald's and Sports Direct have used these contracts, as have the NHS and charities. Zero-hours contracts are higher among young people than other age groups, with 37% of those employed on such contracts aged between 16 and 24.

The CBI (Confederation of British Industry) argue that zero-hours contracts have played an important part in Britain's economic recovery and in having one of the lowest unemployment rates in Europe – in Spain, for example, 50% of those under 25 are unemployed. The CBI states 'flexible contracts provide opportunities for work to help people build careers. They offer a choice to those who want flexibility in the hours they work, such as students, retired people, parents and carers'. The major users of these contracts are in jobs related to accommodation and food, and in administrative and support services. Employers argue that zero-hours contracts provide affordable services to the public and provide employment. Many services in the tourist industry, for example, need this flexibility to survive, and they provide crucial employment in rural areas. The CBI also state that many employees enjoy working with these contracts.

The Trades Union Congress (TUC) argue that many workers on zero-hours contracts are at risk of exploitation and 'for many workers they mean poverty pay and no way of knowing how often they'll be working from week to week'. Again, many workers on zero-hours contracts are prevented from taking other employment even if they are only working for four hours a week as their signed contracts state that employees must be available for work. These contracts mean employers avoid redundancy pay and paying pension contributions, with workers often unable to obtain credit references, loans or mortgages. Workers on these contracts would prefer guaranteed weekly hours and a significant number would prefer more hours. Many workers who achieve limited hours of work are forced to use food banks and to take out loans with very high interest rates.

SOURCE B

Survey findings of employment satisfaction – zero-hours and non-zero-hours workers		
Issue	Zero-hours contract	Non-zero-hours contract
Satisfied with job	60	59
Work–life balance	65	58
Treated unfairly	27	29
Prefer more hours	40	10

SOURCE C

Gross weekly pay and average hours per week: zero-hours and non-zero-hours workers		
Issue	Zero-hours contract	Non-zero-hours contract
Gross weekly pay	250	510
Average no. of hours per week	21	32

Attempt the following question, using only the information from Sources A, B and C.
To what extent is it accurate to state that zero-hours contracts benefit only the employer?

10

Question 3

Study Sources A, B and C then attempt the question that follows.

SOURCE A

Do you support Scottish independence?

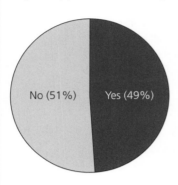

No (51%)   Yes (49%)

Would you back independence if Boris Johnson was Prime Minister?

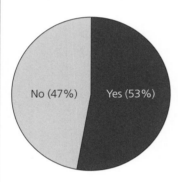

No (47%)   Yes (53%)

Source: a Panelbase survey commissioned by The Sunday Times *(note: in the 2017 general election the newspaper supported the Conservative party).*

Sample size: 1024 Scottish adults, June 2019

SOURCE B

The counting method for the additional member system is described in the White Paper on the Scottish Parliament:

1   Each elector will be entitled to cast two votes: one for a constituency MSP and one for the party of his/her choice.
2   Votes for constituency MSPs will be counted on a first-past-the-post basis.
3   The 56 additional members will be elected in eight seven-member constituencies as follows:
   ▶   The number of votes cast for each party … will be counted
   ▶   The number of votes cast for each party will then be divided by the number of constituency MSPs gained in Parliamentary constituencies … plus one.
   ▶   The party with the highest total after the (above) calculation is done gains the first additional member.
   ▶   The second to seventh additional members are allocated in the same way, but additional members gained are included in the calculations.

Source: extract from Higher Modern Studies textbook UK Politics Today *by Frank Cooney and Peter Fotheringham (Pulse Publications, 2010). This extract provides a factual description of the complexity of AMS and is the system still used today.*

SOURCE C

The Prescription Charges Coalition

The Prescription Charges Coalition brings together more than 30 organisations concerned with the detrimental impact that prescription charges are having on people in England with long-term conditions who are of working age.

Introduction and context

Prescriptions now only carry charges in England, where the system of exemptions, established in 1968 and largely unchanged today, is outdated, arbitrary and inequitable. Certain medical conditions entitle people to exemption from charges, but the majority do not. For those who are diagnosed with a long-term conditions at a young age, this can mean paying for prescriptions on an ongoing basis throughout their working lives.

The Prescription Charges Coalition's latest survey explores the impact of prescription charges on the working lives of people with long-term conditions. More than 5000 people of working age, with a range of long-term conditions, completed the survey. (The report provided both quantitative evidence [survey] and qualitative evidence [interviews with individuals who have to pay for their prescriptions].)

Why do you miss taking your prescription?

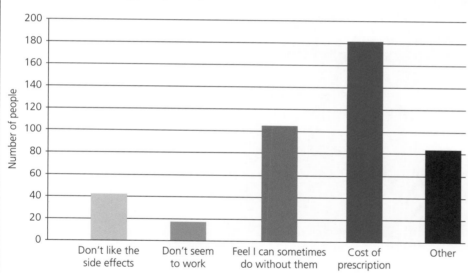

Source: adapted from Paying the Price: Prescription charges and people with long-term conditions *(Prescription Charges Coalition, 2014). This is an English Pressure Group fighting for free prescriptions for those in long-term ill health. (The rest of the United Kingdom provide free prescriptions for all.)*

To what extent are Sources A, B and C reliable?

You must provide an overall conclusion on the most reliable source of information.

8

[END OF PAPER 2]

[END OF PRACTICE PAPER A]

PRACTICE PAPER B

Paper 1

Duration: 1 hour and 45 minutes

Total marks: 52

SECTION 1 – DEMOCRACY IN SCOTLAND AND THE UNITED KINGDOM – 20 marks

Attempt **ONE** Question from 1(a) **OR** 1(b) **OR** 1(c)

SECTION 2 – SOCIAL ISSUES IN THE UNITED KINGDOM – 12 marks

Part A Social inequality

Part B Crime and the law

Attempt **ONE** Question from 2(a) **OR** 2(b) **OR** 2(c) **OR** 2(d)

SECTION 3 – INTERNATIONAL ISSUES – 20 marks

Part C World power

Part D World issues

Attempt **ONE** Question from 3(a) **OR** 3(b) **OR** 3(c) **OR** 3(d)

Read the questions carefully.

You must clearly identify the question number you are attempting.

Use **blue** or **black** ink.

Section 1: Democracy in Scotland and the United Kingdom

Total marks: 20 marks
Attempt **ONE** Question from 1(a) **OR** 1(b) **OR** 1(c)

Question 1

MARKS

(a) To what extent are there differences between the possible alternatives for the future governance of Scotland?

You should refer to Scotland **or** the United Kingdom **or** both in your answer.

20

OR

(b) To what extent are parliamentary representatives effective in holding the Government to account?

You should refer to Scotland **or** the United Kingdom **or** both in your answer.

20

OR

(c) To what extent do some voting systems have more strengths than others?

You should refer to Scotland **or** the United Kingdom **or** both in your answer.

20

Section 2: Social issues in the United Kingdom

Total marks: 12 marks
Attempt **ONE** Question from 2(a) **OR** 2(b) **OR** 2(c) **OR** 2(d)

MARKS

Question 2

Part A: Social inequality

Answers may refer to Scotland or the United Kingdom or both.

(a) Analyse the impact of inequality on a group you have studied.　　12

OR

(b) Evaluate the collectivist viewpoint with regard to inequality.　　12

OR

Part B: Crime and the law

Answers may refer to Scotland or the United Kingdom or both.

(c) Analyse the changes to legal rights of citizens.　　12

OR

(d) Evaluate the impact of crime on victims.　　12

Section 3: International issues

> **Total marks: 20 marks**
> Attempt **ONE** Question from 3(a) **OR** 3(b) **OR** 3(c) **OR** 3(d)

Question 3

Part C: World power

With reference to a world power you have studied:

MARKS

(a) Social inequality can affect a specific group in the world power I have studied.
Discuss.

20

OR

(b) There are many opportunities for democratic participation.
Discuss.

20

OR

Part D: World issues

With reference to a world issue you have studied:

(c) The issue I have studied has many causes.
Discuss.

20

OR

(d) The issue I have studied has an impact on the wider international community.
Discuss.

20

[END OF PAPER 1]

Paper 2

Duration: 1 hour and 15 minutes

Attempt **ALL** questions

Total marks: 28

Read the questions carefully.

You must clearly identify the question number you are attempting.

Use **blue** or **black** ink.

Total marks: 28
Attempt **ALL** questions

Question 1

Study Sources A, B and C then attempt the question which follows.

SOURCE A

The 2015 UK general election

One of the significant features of the 2015 general election was the failure of opinion polls to reflect the actual national election results. All the opinion polls stated that it would be a very close affair – with no party winning an overall majority. Yet the Conservatives won more than 50% of the 650 seats to enable David Cameron to form a Conservative-only Government. The last time the Conservatives had achieved an overall majority was in 1993. The result was a personal triumph for David Cameron – he had been criticised for not securing a clear Conservative victory in the 2010 election. Now there would be no further coalition Government with the Liberal Democrats.

However, opinion polls were far more accurate when it came to Scotland. They all predicted a clear victory for the SNP and a complete sea-change in the voting habits of the Scottish electorate. In fact, the 'tartan tsunami' completely swept away Labour dominance. Support for Labour and Liberal Democrat candidates collapsed across Scotland. The Conservatives retained their one seat, but experienced a decline in their percentage of votes.

The 2015 general election witnessed a complete collapse of support for the Liberal Democrats – in terms of votes UKIP became the third-largest party. The Liberal Democrats were severely punished by the electorate for having been in a coalition Government with the Conservatives. Their leader, Nick Clegg, resigned after the election. Ed Miliband, the Labour leader, also resigned after what he described as a 'very disappointing night'. In terms of votes UKIP did best in England with 14.1% of the electorate's votes and worst in Scotland, winning less than 2% of the votes.

It was a strange election which highlighted the inconsistencies and shortcomings of the First-Past-the-Post (FPTP) system. Labour increased its percentage of votes but suffered a loss in seats. UKIP gained over 3.8 million votes but this was not reflected in seats gained. In Scotland the Unionist parties – Labour, the Conservatives and Liberal Democrats – gained combined significant voting support, yet only received 5% of the seats. The Green Party won over 1 million votes and retained their one seat. No wonder the Electoral Reform Society stated that 'this was the most disproportionate result in British election history, and once again FPTP has failed to accurately reflect the wishes of the British electorate'. The make-up of Parliament clearly demonstrates the massive divide in voting behaviour between Scotland and England.

SOURCE B

Election results by area (Great Britain) and change from 2010

	Con	Labour	Lib Dem	Others	Total
England					
Seats	319	206	6	2	533
Change	22	15	−37	0	–
Share of vote	36.8%	30.4%	7.9%	24.9%	
Change	1.5%	3.5%	−16.0%	13.5%	–
Wales					
Seats	11	25	1	3	40
Change	3	−1	−2	0	–
Share of vote	27.5%	62.5%	2.5%	7.5%	
Change	1.1%	0.6%	−13.6%	14.5%	–
Scotland					
				SNP	
Seats	1	1	1	56	59
Change	0	−40	−10	50	–
Share of vote	14.9%	24.3%	7.5%	50.1%	
Change	−1.8%	−7.4%	−17.7%	30.9%	–

SOURCE C

UK general election results 2015

Party	Seats	Change from 2010	Seats %	Votes %
Conservatives	331	25	50.9	36.9
Labour	232	−26	35.7	30.4
SNP	56	50	8.6	4.7
UKIP	1	0	0.2	12.6
Liberal Democrats	8	−49	1.2	7.9

Attempt the following question, using only the information in Sources A, B and C.

What conclusions can be drawn about the results of the 2015 general election?

You must draw conclusions about:

▶ the fairness of the FPTP electoral system

▶ the performance of the UK political parties in England and Wales compared to Scotland

▶ the accuracy of opinion polls compared to the actual result.

You must also make an overall conclusion on the performance of UK political parties in the 2015 general election.

10

Question 2

Study Sources A, B and C then attempt the question that follows.

SOURCE A

'ANC once again won the South African election'

In May 2014 elections were held to elect a national Government and regional Governments for the nine provinces of South Africa. The African National Congress (ANC) comfortably won the election, as it has done in the four previous elections. A spokesperson for the party stated that, once again, the election witnessed 'an outstanding victory for the ANC across the country', winning 11 million of the 18 million votes cast and over 60% of the 400 seats. The ANC is the party that ended white rule in 1994 under the leadership of Nelson Mandela.

The ANC percentage of votes in 2014 was its lowest figure ever. In addition, the ANC retained control of eight of the nine provinces, gaining more than 70% of the votes in three of the provinces, namely the Eastern Cape, Limpopo and Mpumalanga (the three poorest and least educated of the nine provinces). In contrast, the ANC's worst results were in the two wealthiest provinces – Gauteng and Western Cape. The ANC failed to win back the Western Cape, which it had lost in 2009 national elections.

The Democratic Alliance (DA) achieved its best ever result, and more importantly, it retained control of the Western Cape Province. In total, the DA obtained over 4 million national votes, with most of the 1 million new voters coming from middle-class black Africans. The DA has increased its support in every general election. Its main supporters are white people, those of mixed race and Asians – but as stated, it has the support of a growing number of black African voters.

South Africa uses a proportional representation (PR) system called the Party List. This system encourages the formation of new parties, and several participated in the 2014 election. The most successful of the new parties was the Economic Freedom Fighters (EFF), which won 1.2 million (6.4%) of the votes. Its leader, Julius Malema, is a former member of the ANC and his far-left policies appealed to sections of the poorest groups in the country. The EFF became the main opposition in the provinces of Limpopo and North West.

Electoral turnout was a healthy 73.4%, although this was down from the 77.3% turnout of the 2009 election. However, about 7 million voters chose not to vote and over 62% of those aged 18–19, the 'born-free generation', did not vote. This suggests that many South Africans are disillusioned with the ANC and with politics in general. The growing gap between wealthy and poor blacks, and the accusations of widespread corruption within the ANC, perhaps explains this growing discontent.

SOURCE B

South African National Election results 2014: selected parties

Party	Percentage of total vote	% Change since 2009	Number of MPs	+/– from 2009
ANC	62.1	–3.8	249	–15
DA	22.2	5.5	89	22
IFP	2.4	–2.1	10	–8
EFF*	6.35	6.3	25	–
COPE	0.7	–6.9	3	–27

*New party

SOURCE C

Voting support in selected provinces 2014 and % change since 2009

Province	ANC (% change)	DA (% change)	IFP (% change)	EFF (% change)*
Gauteng	53.5 (–9.9)	30.7 (+8.8)	0.8 (–0.7)	10.3 (–)
Western Cape	32.8 (+1.3)	59.3 (+1.3)	0.01 (–0.9)	2.1 (–)
Limpopo	78.6 (–6.2)	6.5 (+3.1)	0.01 (–)	10.7 (–)
KwaZulu-Natal	64.5 (+1.6)	12.7 (+3.6)	10.8 (–11.6)	1.8 (–)

*New party

Attempt the following question, using only the information in Sources A, B and C.

To what extent is it accurate to state that the results of the 2014 election were an outstanding victory for the ANC across all of South Africa?

10

Question 3

Study Sources A, B and C then attempt the question that follows.

SOURCE A

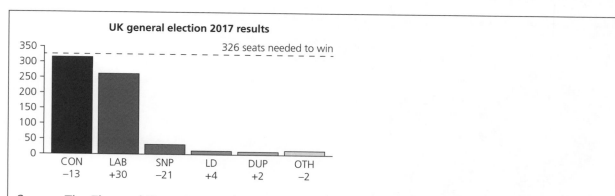

Source: The Electoral Commission. This is the election commission of the United Kingdom and it is an independent body which sets standards for how elections should be conducted.

SOURCE B

17 August at 14:34 ·

Fantastic victory for us in the Beacon and Radnorshire by-election!

Rejoice, the Liberal Democrats are once again a major force in the country. Our stunning victory in this Welsh by-election has humiliated the Conservatives who have lost this seat. We have overturned an 8038 majority to beat the Conservatives by 1425 votes.

Labour just managed to save their deposit and the Brexit party did not fare much better.

LIBERAL DEMOCRATS: 13,826 VOTES AND 43.5% OF THE VOTES

THE BREXITEERS: ONLY AROUND 3000 VOTES

FIGHT TO REMAIN IN THE EU!

64   2 comments 6 shares

Like   Comment   Share

Source: extract from the Facebook page of a Liberal Democrat supporter, August 2019.

SOURCE C

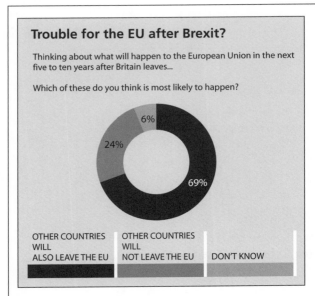

Trouble for the EU after Brexit?

Thinking about what will happen to the European Union in the next five to ten years after Britain leaves...

Which of these do you think is most likely to happen?

6%

24%

69%

OTHER COUNTRIES WILL ALSO LEAVE THE EU

OTHER COUNTRIES WILL NOT LEAVE THE EU

DON'T KNOW

Source: Ipsos MORI interviewed a representative quota sample of 1000 adults aged 18+ across Scotland (2017).

Attempt the following question, using only the information in Sources A, B and C.

To what extent are Sources A, B and C reliable?

You must provide an overall conclusion on the most reliable source of information.

8

[END OF PAPER 2]

[END OF PRACTICE PAPER B]

Paper 1

Section 1: Democracy in Scotland and the United Kingdom

1(a) You can be credited in a number of ways *up to a maximum of 12 marks*.

Credit responses that make reference to:

▶ groups and methods used that influence decision-making

▶ analysis of influence of different pressure groups.

Credit reference to aspects of the following:

▶ Cause or interest groups can promote a single issue (for example, Friends of the Earth) or those that represent sectional interests (for example, trade unions, UNISON). Groups with financial means and larger membership and with a cause that has government support are more successful.

▶ Insider and outsider groups. Insider groups such as the BMA have excellent ties with government decision-makers and are included in private discussions. Outsider groups lack official recognition and have to convert/mobilise the public or take action to assert influence – for example, students protesting against the raising of student fees used marches, petitions and contacting MPs.

▶ Examples of successful action may include: the Gurkhas winning full citizenship rights in the UK; also the Scottish legal profession persuaded the Scottish Government to delay the repeal of corroboration in Scottish court cases. However, pressure groups can be in conflict and may use UK or European courts to block government action. The Scottish whisky industry has challenged (and blocked) the introduction of minimum alcohol pricing in Scotland.

▶ Examples of failed pressure group activity: tension within the coalition Government of 2010–2015 ensured groups campaigning for an elected UK second chamber did not achieve the promised reform, as a Conservative backbench revolt led to the House of Lords reform bill being dropped.

Possible approaches to answering the question:

Response 1

The methods that a pressure group uses will depend on its relationship with the Government. If it is respected and has significant influence, it may work directly with the Government. The British Medical Association (BMA) and the Scottish legal establishment are examples of insider groups.

(Total 2 marks: 1 mark KU and 1 mark analysis)

Response 2

The methods that a pressure group uses will depend on its relationship with the Government. If it is respected and has significant influence it may work directly with the Government. The BMA is an example of an insider group supporting the introduction of minimum pricing of alcohol. The BMA, given its informed and expert knowledge, is regularly contacted by the Government and contributes to government health promotional campaigns, such as moderation in drinking and participation in exercise. This highlights the success of an insider pressure group in influencing government decisions.

(Total 4 marks: 2 marks KU and 2 marks analysis)

Response 3

In contrast to insider groups such as the CBI, pressure groups who have goals that are out of step with government policies usually have limited influence. They are unlikely to be consulted by the Government and will have limited contact with the Government. These outsider groups try to mobilise public opinion and achieve media attention through marches and leaflets. In 2010 the National Union of Students of England and Wales in England marched in London against a rise in tuition fees. Unfortunately, a minority of marchers began a riot, smashing shop windows and attacking the police. The protest did not force a government U-turn, and in fact the march damaged the image of the students. Therefore, outsider pressure groups are at a complete disadvantage in influencing decision-making compared to insider groups.

(Total 5 marks: 3 marks KU and 2 marks analysis)

1(b) You can be credited in a number of ways **up to a maximum of 12 marks**.

Credit responses that make reference to:

▶ the impact on a range of issues

▶ analysis of impact of leaving the EU.

Credit reference to aspects of the following:

▶ Economic savings – the UK pays an annual net contribution of around £8 million; freedom to negotiate trade agreements.

▶ Sovereignty – the UK Parliament will once again have full control; EU laws, regulations and directives on issues such as fisheries, farming, environment, energy and immigration will no longer apply.

▶ International standing – the UK will not be overshadowed by the EU and will regain its former status.

▶ Constitutional – Scotland and Northern Ireland voted to remain in the EU and the possibility of a no-deal Brexit could lead to the breakup of the UK. Prime Minister May's agreement was rejected by Parliament.

▶ Security – safer as part of an EU that combats terrorism together. Europol membership allows EU-wide sharing of intelligence and cross-border support.

▶ Loss of free movement and free market – over a million Britons live in other EU countries and around half of all UK trade is conducted with the EU.

Possible approaches to answering the question:

Response 1

The UK will gain back its national sovereignty and the UK Parliament and courts would not need to enforce EU directives.

(Total 1 mark: KU)

Response 2

The UK will gain back its national sovereignty, and the UK Parliament and courts would not need to enforce EU directives. Decisions that impact on British citizens are made by faceless bureaucrats in Brussels and are destroying British values and traditions.

(Total 2 marks: 1 mark KU, 1 mark analysis)

Response 3

The UK will gain back its national sovereignty and the UK Parliament and courts would not need to enforce EU directives. Decisions that impact on British citizens are made by faceless bureaucrats in Brussels and are destroying British values and traditions. British taxpayers are subsidising French and other European farmers. The EU is a 'gravy train' for those who work in it – the total budget for EU administration is estimated at £35 billion a year. The European Parliament has no real powers and the EU has a democracy deficit.

(Total 4 marks: 2 marks KU, 2 marks analysis)

1(c) You can be credited in a number of ways **up to a maximum of 12 marks**.

Credit responses that make reference to:

▶ factors which influence voting behaviour

▶ evaluation of different factors which influence voting behaviour.

Credit reference to aspects of the following Scottish and/or UK dimensions:

▶ Importance of social class and recent trends – the period between 1979 and today is described as one of declining party identification and partisan de-alignment. Many traditional Labour voters switched to the SNP in the 2011 Scottish Parliament Election and again in the 2015 general election.

▶ Other long-term factors such as age, ethnicity and gender. Clear link between age and party support – the young are more likely to vote Labour and older voters to choose the Conservatives. Ethnic minority voters are more likely to vote Labour. However, ethnicity can be affected by short-term issues such as the Labour Government's support for the Iraq War.

▶ Regional variations – a north–south divide is evident with anti-Conservative support highest in Scotland, Wales and the north of England. The Conservatives' support is highest in southern England and English suburbs and rural areas. Link here to social class. Also, social class is more relevant in England than Scotland.

▶ The 2015 and 2017 general elections and rise of national/cultural factors – the SNP in Scotland and UKIP in England.

- Short-term influences such as party policies, image of party leaders and issue voting. Leadership of Ed Miliband became a key issue in the 2015 general election and Theresa May in the 2017 general election.
- Role of media in influencing voters – including newspapers, television, radio, etc. Also, growing influence of new media. However, the success of Nick Clegg in the 2010 party leaders' debate did not translate into more votes for the Liberal Democrats.
- Credit will be given to candidates who show links between factors.

Possible approaches to answering the question:

Response 1

There is an important link between social class and voting behaviour. Social class is a measure of a person's status in society – for example, professional people such as doctors or lawyers (social class A/B) or semi-skilled or unskilled (social class D/E). Statistics from elections would suggest that A/B voters are far more likely to vote Conservative, with around 43% of this group (the largest percentage) voting Conservative in the 2015 UK general election. On the other hand, around 40% of D/E voters (the largest percentage) opted for Labour in 2015. Today, it is argued that around 40% of voters continue to vote in line with their social class.

(Total 3 marks: 2 marks KU, 1 mark evaluation)

Response 2

In Scotland, the image of Alex Salmond and Nicola Sturgeon has been very positive. Both leaders have often been seen as energetic, competent and statesmanlike. Even when the *Sun* newspaper attacked the SNP and Salmond in the 2007 Scottish Parliament Election, the SNP went on to become the largest party, with Salmond as the new First Minister, demonstrating that image is sometimes more important than newspaper support.

(Total 3 marks: 2 marks KU, 1 mark evaluation)

Response 3

Most electors today obtain their political information from the media (either 'old media' such as newspapers or TV, or 'new media' such as the internet or social media) and as such the media plays an important part in shaping the views of the electorate. For example, the stories that newspapers select or their choice of headlines, pictures or editorials can all have a 'drip, drip' effect on readers, influencing their politics over time. In the UK general election of 2015, the *Sun*'s and other newspapers' repeated criticism of Labour leader Ed Miliband was said to have cost Labour votes. Politicians and political parties would certainly agree with this view that newspapers influence voters as they often aim to keep newspaper owners or editors 'on side'. However, it has been argued that the influence of newspapers has been overstated. For example, many readers are unaware of or ignore the political stance of their newspaper.

(Total 4 marks: 2 marks KU, 2 marks evaluation)

Response 4

Overall, there are many different interlinked factors that affect voting behaviour. Some factors, such as social class, age and geography, overlap and are therefore difficult to measure separately. However, it's clear that these long-term factors taken together continue to be an important influence on voting behaviour even if dealignment has reduced the importance of class-based voting. The rise of nationalism in Scotland and cultural identity in England has further weakened the influence of social class. In the same way, it is difficult to measure the overall influence of the media/new media on voting behaviour. There is little doubt that people gain most of their political information from the media, but it is impossible to identify one aspect or another of the media, for example the newspaper a voter reads, as being the single most important reason why they support any one party. However, most political commentators would agree that as the media becomes an ever greater influence in people's lives, it is expected that the impact of the media, particularly new media, will increase.

(Total 4 marks: overall evaluative comment that addresses the question)

Section 2: Social issues in the United Kingdom

2(a) You can be credited in a number of ways **up to a maximum of 20 marks.**

Award marks where candidates refer to aspects of the following:

▶ government policies introduced to reduce inequality for this group

▶ an evaluation of the success of these policies.

Candidates may refer to:

▶ young/old

▶ gender/ethnicity

▶ social/economic status

▶ disability.

Credit reference to aspects of the following:

▶ The elderly:
  - wide range of Welfare State provision including state benefits, housing, health and personal services
  - reference to official reports and statistics – for example, poverty levels among pensioners, demographic trends
  - poverty reduction targets achieved, with a significant decline in elderly poverty
  - proposed changes to welfare including the new state pension introduced in April 2016
  - pension age being raised – by 2020 both men and women will receive state pension only when they turn 67
  - debate over the continuation of universal benefits for the elderly: free TV licence for those 75+ to be means-tested
  - Scottish government action – free personal care for the elderly, free bus travel around Scotland.

Possible approaches to answering the question:

Response 1

Inequalities exist among the elderly in terms of good health, income and quality of life. The NHS spends a significant amount of its budget on the elderly. The Government provide for their material needs through state pensions, pension credits and other benefits. A new state pension system was introduced in April 2016.

(Total 2 marks: both KU)

Response 2

One economic reason for financial inequality among the elderly is the provision or non-provision of a work pension. The elderly who depend only on the state pension can be pushed into poverty with the rising cost of food and heating their home. In recent years fuel and food prices have increased significantly. Government have addressed this inequality issue through means-tested benefits such as pension credits, Cold Weather Payment, Housing Benefit and Council Tax Reduction. The proportion of pensioners living in poverty has fallen in recent years from 26% in 2001 to 14% in 2014. This is clear evidence of progress. However, many elderly still experience fuel poverty.

(Total 4 marks: 2 marks KU, 2 marks evaluation)

Response 3

The Government's austerity cuts have had little impact on the elderly. The Coalition Government, as a result of the 2008 economic crisis, made savings of £81 billion in public spending. While Child Benefit is now means-tested, the state pension and the winter fuel allowance are still given to all elderly regardless of income. While annual payment increases to the unemployed have been reduced in real terms, the state pension is protected and will rise annually by 2.5% or the rate of inflation, whichever is higher. However, some critics question this protection of the wealthy elderly and feel that they should take their share of the cuts. The elderly would argue that the low rate of interest rates has reduced the value of their savings.

(Total 4 marks: 2 marks KU, 2 marks evaluation)

2(b) You can be credited in a number of ways **up to a maximum of 20 marks**.

Award marks where candidates refer to aspects of the following:

▶ the main causes of health inequalities

▶ an evaluation of the main causes of health inequalities.

Candidates may refer to:

▶ evidence of health inequalities and their link to poverty rates

▶ impact of poverty on health: poor housing, effect on mental health

▶ Harry Burns' research on 'biology of poverty'

▶ lifestyle choices – smoking, alcohol, diet and exercise.

Possible approaches to answering the question:

Response 1

There is clear evidence that poverty is an important explanation for health inequalities. Numerous government reports, from the Black Report onwards, highlight the link between deprivation and poor health.

(Total 1 mark: KU)

Response 2

There is clear evidence that poverty is an important explanation for health inequalities. Numerous government reports, from the Black Report onwards, highlight the link between deprivation and poor health. An NHS Scotland 2018 report revealed that the poorest 10% of Scots are three times more likely to die prematurely compared to the 10% who are most affluent. The report concludes that a third of early deaths and ill health could be avoided if the whole population had the same life circumstances as the people who live in the more affluent areas.

(Total 3 marks: 2 marks KU, 1 mark analysis)

Response 3

It is self-evident that poor lifestyle choices such as smoking, drinking to excess and poor diet impact on an individual's health. Daily alcohol consumption in Scotland is 25% higher than in England. Obesity is also a lifestyle choice, and more Scots are becoming obese. It is estimated that over 2000 Scots die every year as a direct result of obesity. However, it is clear that obesity and smoking and alcohol abuse are social class and poverty issues – 35% of people living in the most deprived areas smoke cigarettes, compared to only 10% in the least deprived areas. It is difficult to make good lifestyle choices when you are unemployed, living in poor housing and in a deprived area.

(Total 4 marks: 2 marks KU, 1 mark analysis, 1 mark evaluation)

2(c) You can be credited in a number of ways **up to a maximum of 20 marks**.

Credit responses that make reference to:

▶ links between poverty and crime

▶ evaluation of other factors that cause criminal behaviour.

Credit reference to aspects of the following:

▶ evidence of the link between poverty and criminal behaviour – most deprived regions experience significantly more crime/violent crime than affluent areas and more than half of Scotland's prison population have home addresses in the most deprived areas

▶ evidence of the link between poverty and lack of educational attainment, high unemployment and mental health issues

▶ other factors including biological factors ('criminal gene'), 'bad parenting', gender, alcohol and drugs, peer pressure/youth gangs, etc.

▶ criminological theories, for example, positivists (crime caused by the way people are and/or the environment) and classical theories (crime is a choice/free will).

Possible approaches to answering the question:

Response 1

There is a clear link between poverty/deprivation and criminal behaviour. The Scottish Index of Multiple Deprivation (SIMD) shows that the most deprived areas experience more crime than other more affluent areas. For example, Glasgow, Renfrewshire and West Dunbartonshire have some of the highest levels of deprivation, and as a result suffer the greatest levels of crime, including violent crime.

(Total 2 marks: 1 mark KU, 1 mark evaluation)

Response 2

Gender also is a key cause of criminal behaviour. Recent Scottish prison statistics stated that the prison service holds about 7700 prisoners, of whom only around 500 are female. Over 80% of violent crimes are committed by men. Most women are convicted of non-violent crimes, which can lead to prison sentences if they cannot afford to pay the fines imposed. There is a clear link to poverty, with the majority of women prisoners having postcodes identified within areas of high deprivation.

(Total 3 marks: 2 marks KU, 1 mark evaluation)

Response 3

As well as social deprivation, there are a great many other explanations as to why crime occurs. One explanation is so-called 'bad parenting'. This explanation talks about parents as poor role models who do not enforce boundaries as to what is right or wrong. They often have a poor attitude to authority and this is passed on to their children. Government statistics show that an average of 43% of those in prison have had other family members in prison. Crime, it would appear, does run in families.

(Total 3 marks: 2 marks KU, 1 mark evaluation)

2(d) You can be credited in a number of ways **up to a maximum of 20 marks**.

Credit responses that make reference to:

▶ evaluation of community-based punishments
▶ evaluation of rehabilitation programmes in prisons.

Credit reference to aspects of the following:

▶ aims and purposes of prison – punishment, deterrence, protection and rehabilitation
▶ increase in number of prisoners across the UK; highest crime rates in Europe
▶ issue of women prisoners in Scotland and England – increase and conditions
▶ high rates of recidivism (the tendency to reoffend) for short-term prisoners
▶ problems in prisons which hinder rehabilitation – overcrowding, drug use, mental health issues
▶ recognition by the UK and Scottish Governments that prisons are failing for short-term sentences
▶ cuts to prison budgets have led to a greater use of alternatives.

Possible approaches to answering the question:

Response 1

The total number of prisoners held in Scottish prisons in 2018 was on average 7500. Many prisoners have a background of poor mental health and drug addiction. Their mental health needs are not being met and many women prisoners self-harm – one in three women in prison are on suicide watch.

(Total 2 marks: 1 mark KU, 1 mark evaluation)

Response 2

One reason that prisons find it difficult to rehabilitate prisoners and thus reduce crime is because of overcrowding. Chronic overcrowding stretches prison resources and can lead to tension between prison officers and prisoners. In 2013 the English prison services riot squad was called out 203 times – up from 129 in 2012. Conditions in prisons in England and Wales are worsening as Victorian prisons are being closed down to save money – 18 have been closed or repurposed since 2010. Swansea prison has almost twice as many inmates as it was designed to house.

(Total 4 marks: 3 marks KU, 1 mark evaluation)

Response 3

One reason that prisons find it difficult to rehabilitate prisoners is because of overcrowding. Chronic overcrowding stretches prison resources and can lead to tension between prison officers and prisoners. In 2013 the English prison services riot squad was called out 203 times – up from 129 in 2012. Conditions in prisons in England and Wales are worsening as Victorian prisons are being closed down to save money – 18 have been closed or repurposed since 2010. Swansea prison has almost twice as many inmates as it was designed to house. This explains why overcrowding is a factor in increasing the rate of reoffending – 75% of short-term prisoners are likely to reoffend. Staffing has also been reduced. Prisons have been forced to reduce their budgets by a quarter, leading to a significant reduction in the number of prison officers. Since 2000, the ratio of officers to prisoners has fallen from one in three to one in five in England. This makes it more difficult for staff to escort prisoners to workshops and classrooms – all essential parts of rehabilitation.

(Total 5 marks: 3 marks KU, 2 marks evaluation)

Section 3: International issues

3(a) You can be credited in a number of ways **up to a maximum of 20 marks.**

Credit responses that make reference to:

▶ the role of world power within the international community

▶ analysis/evaluation of its international influence

▶ balanced overall evaluative comment on the extent of its influence

▶ provide a clear and coherent line of argument.

Credit reference to aspects of the following – world power: China:

▶ leading role as a permanent member of the UN Security Council

▶ participates in UN peacekeeping operations

▶ relationship with and future role in negotiations with North Korea

▶ impact of USA/China diplomatic relations

▶ investment in African countries and elsewhere

▶ growing importance of China in the world economy (second to the USA and expected to surpass it)

▶ member of the G20

▶ member of the World Bank and IMF.

Possible approaches to answering the question about world power: China:

Response 1

China is the biggest contributor to peacekeeping missions among the UN Security Council's permanent five members and it takes part in anti-piracy patrols off the Horn of Africa.

(Total 1 mark: KU)

Response 2

China has a huge influence over the world. Not only is it a nuclear superpower, but it is also a permanent member of the UN Security Council. This means that it has the power of veto over any resolutions drafted to the Council in dealing with armed conflict. An example of China using this power was in 2012 and again in 2014, when China, along with Russia, vetoed UN involvement in Syria when its people were attempting to topple President Assad. This was against the will of other Security Council members such as the UK and the USA and shows the power that China has.

(Total 4 marks: 2 marks KU, 2 marks analysis/evaluation)

Response 3

China has a huge influence over the world. Not only is it a nuclear superpower but it is also a permanent member of the UN Security Council. This means that it has the power of veto over any resolutions drafted to the Council in dealing with armed conflict. An example of China using this power was in 2012 and again in 2014, when China, along with Russia, vetoed UN involvement in Syria when its people were attempting to topple President Assad. This was against the will of other Security Council members such as the UK and the USA and shows the power that China has.

China is the second-largest economic power, behind the USA. However, it is expected to surpass the USA within a decade as its manufacturing base continues to grow from strength to strength. One area of the world which is heavily influenced by China's economic power is Africa. Over the past 20 years China has invested heavily in trade deals with countries on the African continent. Trade with Africa surpassed £120 billion in 2012, and in the past two years China has given more loans to countries in Africa than the World Bank has given. China has boosted employment in Africa and made basic goods like shoes and radios more affordable. However, there has been strong criticism over the lack of fairness and safety of African workers who work for Chinese companies in Africa.

(Total 6 marks: 4 marks KU, 2 marks analysis/evaluation)

Credit reference to aspects of the following – world power: USA:

▶ leading member of NATO, biggest contributor – including the example of mobilising European action in the Ukraine crisis

▶ leading role in UN, permanent member of UN Security Council and biggest UN contributor

▶ military interventions – example of involvement in Afghanistan and Iraq, and leading the fight against ISIS

▶ largest economy in the world and foremost military power; US Navy projects, US military power around the globe

- ▶ role in Middle East and support for Israel
- ▶ member of G8 and G20
- ▶ nuclear superpower
- ▶ impact on the USA of the emergence of China as a regional power in Asia.

Possible approaches to answering the question – world power: USA:

Response 1

The USA's role as the only superpower ensures that its international involvement and influence covers the entire globe, with involvement that covers Europe, Africa, Asia and South America.

(Total 1 mark: KU)

Response 2

The USA is an extremely influential world power, with the world's largest economy and unrivalled military strength. The USA is the only military superpower. In recent years the USA has spent more on defence than the next nine nations combined, although the USA is having to cut back on defence spending as it can no longer afford to spend as much. The USA dominates NATO, although all members are supposedly equal, and it used its influence to ensure that NATO played its part in Afghanistan. During the Afghan War the USA contributed by far the most hardware and troops, with over 100,000 US soldiers in the country a few years ago. Most commentators would agree that NATO needs the USA, but the USA does not always need NATO.

(Total 4 marks: 2 marks KU, 2 marks analysis/evaluation)

3(b) You can be credited in a number of ways **up to a maximum of 20 marks**.

Credit responses that make reference to:

- ▶ the political system of the world power
- ▶ analysis/evaluation of the ways in which the political system effectively protects the rights of all of its citizens
- ▶ analysis/evaluation of its international influence.

Credit responses that provide:

- ▶ balanced overall evaluative comment on the extent of its effectiveness
- ▶ a clear and coherent line of argument.

Credit reference to aspects of the following – world power: South Africa:

- ▶ South Africa is a well-established democracy with an extensive Bill of Rights, fair and free elections, high voter turnout, a fair electoral system and many political parties to vote for.
- ▶ Regular elections are held every five years and the president can only serve two terms. The Party List electoral system is highly proportionate as the number of votes a party wins will be roughly the same as the number of seats they get in Parliament.
- ▶ At the 2014 general election, voters could vote for a range of parties – the ANC led by Jacob Zuma and Democratic Alliance now led by Helen Zille. There were also seven new parties, such as the Economic Freedom Fighters.
- ▶ One view is that the ANC has too much power and that South Africa is moving towards being a one-party state. This makes it far from being fair and democratic.
- ▶ The ANC controls eight out of the nine provinces and only the Democratic Alliance in Western Cape offer an alternative.

Possible approaches to answering the question – world power: South Africa:

Response 1

South Africa has all the features of a successful democracy, with national elections held every five years and voters allowed to choose among a range of political parties. It has a written constitution which includes a bill of rights and also provides for an independent judiciary to interpret the legality of government actions.

(Total 2 marks: both KU)

Response 2

The electoral system strengthens the president's powers and stifles debate and opposition within the ruling party. The Party List system gives President Zuma great power as he must approve the ANC candidates. This means that ANC politicians are more loyal to their leader than to the voters, as they fear being moved down the list. In the past, ANC politicians have been removed for criticising ANC policies. Zuma fired Trevor Ngane for criticising his privatisation policies. The president appoints not only his ministers but also eight of the nine premiers of the provincial governments.

(Total 4 marks: 2 marks KU, 2 marks analysis/evaluation)

Response 3

It can be argued that South Africa's political system is democratic as free and fair elections are held and the public can choose from a range of political parties. It has a liberal constitution and the people's rights are protected by a still-independent judiciary – the Constitutional Court. The country still has a free press and the Government can be criticised and challenged. However, the domination, corruption and arrogance of the ANC could lead to a one-party state. Jacob Zuma has stated that the ANC will rule 'until Jesus returns'. Legislation has been passed through Parliament to weaken the freedom of the press and to prevent newspapers from exposing the corruption of the ANC leadership. Zuma's control of the Public Prosecution Department and state security are worrying signs of a step towards dictatorship. His resignation offers hope of greater democracy. Respected figures such as Desmond Tutu have openly attacked the corruption of the ANC and endorse the view that there are two types of ANC leaders – those who were in jail (under white rule) and those who should be in jail.

(Total 4 marks: balanced conclusion with detailed evaluative comment)

3(c) You can be credited in a number of ways **up to a maximum of 20 marks.**

Credit responses that make reference to:

▶ consequences of this issue on those affected

▶ analysis/evaluation of the consequences of this issue.

Credit reference to aspects of the following:

▶ world issue: international terrorism (UN/NATO)

▶ world issue: development in Africa (UN agencies/NGOs)

▶ world issue: nuclear proliferation (UN)

▶ world issue: global economic crisis (EU/World Bank/IMF).

Possible approaches to answering the question – development issues in Africa:

Response 1

One international issue is the lack of development in many countries in Africa. The lack of available and affordable healthcare and education are said to be two of the most important factors limiting development. For example, in Malawi life expectancy is low (54 years), and one in six people cannot read or write.

(Total 1 mark: KU)

Response 2

One international issue is the lack of development in many countries in Africa. The lack of available and affordable healthcare and education are said to be two of the most important factors limiting development. For example, in Malawi life expectancy is low (54 years) and illiteracy rates are high (one in six people cannot read or write). However, in recent years many African countries have seen real improvements in standards of living, many experiencing faster economic growth than countries in Europe. Free from civil war, the people of countries such as Mozambique and Angola have been able to invest in schools and medical clinics and have made progress in reducing illnesses such as HIV/AIDS or increasing the number of children in primary school.

(Total 4 marks: 3 marks KU, 1 mark analysis/evaluation)

Response 3

Overall, development in African countries has been mixed if, for example, measured against the UN's Millennium Development Goals. Countries that have experienced good government and have been free from war, such as Tanzania and Ghana, have made sustained progress. However, where the Government have been accused of corruption (Nigeria) or where there has been conflict (Sudan), there has been much less progress.

(Total 2 marks: balanced overall comment)

3(d) You can be credited in a number of ways **up to a maximum of 20 marks**.

Credit responses that make reference to:

▶ actions taken by international organisations to resolve a world issue

▶ the effectiveness of these actions.

Credit reference to aspects of the following:

▶ world issue: international terrorism (UN/NATO)

▶ world issue: development in Africa (UN agencies/NGOs)

▶ world issue: nuclear proliferation (UN)

▶ world issue: crisis in Ukraine.

Possible approaches to answering the question – development issues in Africa:

Response 1

Lack of development in African countries is a long-standing issue caused by social, economic and political problems. For example, it is estimated that 30% of Africa's 180 million children do not attend school. International organisations such as the UN have tried to resolve these issues through aid projects and UN peacekeepers, which have had varying levels of success.

(Total 2 marks: 1 mark KU, 1 mark evaluation)

Response 2

The work the UN does in developing nations in Africa is vital in supporting development. UNICEF works to improve and protect the lives of children in developing nations by trying to ensure all children receive their human rights, such as access to education and hospitals. UNICEF has built 415 new classrooms in the remotest parts of Mali and Burkina Faso so thousands of children can receive an education. UNICEF has also targeted the shortage of teachers. These areas are now prospering, with an educated youth able to contribute to society and build an economy in the future. However, as much as UNICEF is making progress in many countries in Africa, work still needs to be done to tackle the inadequacy of education provision and the shocking rates of non-attendance, especially for girls at secondary level.

(Total 5 marks: 3 marks KU, 2 marks evaluation)

Response 3

Lack of development in many countries of Africa is very difficult to resolve. Three important factors which limit development are the lack of healthcare and education, and tension between different tribal groups.

(Total 1 mark: KU)

Response 4

Almost all of the countries in the continent of Africa are developing countries. There are various causes which contribute to the lack of development, which vary from country to country. The first cause of under-development is debt. Many African governments have borrowed money from the International Monetary Fund (IMF) or the World Bank to finance development. However, at times this money has been misspent and these institutions attach high interest rates to their loans that result in massive repayments for many years. This prevents countries spending enough money on education and health. In 2013, Angola's debt was over $18 billion.

(Total 4 marks: 2 marks KU, 2 marks analysis/evaluation)

Response 5

A further cause of underdevelopment is armed conflict. Armed conflict can tear a country apart and have devastating effects on social and economic development. Over the last few decades many African nations have been locked in civil war. Continuing conflict in Sudan has driven 2 million people from their homes and killed more than 200,000 people. Governments struggle to function properly in war-torn countries and to fulfil their basic role of running the country for the benefit of the people.

(Total 4 marks: 2 marks KU, 2 marks analysis/evaluation)

Paper 2

1 You can be credited in a number of ways **up to a maximum of 10 marks.**

Possible approaches to answering the question – the link between the popular vote and Electoral College vote in the 2016 election:

Response 1

There is no guarantee that the candidate who wins the most votes will win the most Electoral College votes. Source A states that Clinton won the popular vote, but Trump won the most Electoral College votes, winning 306 votes compared to Clinton's 232.

(Total 2 marks: overall conclusion supported by detailed evidence from Source A)

Response 2

There is no guarantee that the candidate who wins the most votes will win the most Electoral College votes. Source A states that Clinton won the popular vote, but Trump won the most Electoral College votes. The popular vote is not shared proportionally in each state in terms of Electoral College votes and this explains why Trump gained a clear victory in the Electoral College vote, winning 306 votes compared to Clinton's 232. In contrast, Trump only won 46.2% of the popular vote while Clinton won 48.1%. She received 65.5 million votes compared to 62.8 million votes for Trump – a clear majority.

(Total 3 marks: overall conclusion supported by detailed evidence)

Possible approaches to answering the question – the influence of age and ethnicity on voting behaviour in the 2016 election:

Response 3

The elderly and white non-Hispanics were more likely to vote for Trump and younger voters and ethnic minorities were more likely to vote for Clinton.

(Total 0 marks: conclusion with no supporting evidence)

Response 4

The elderly and white non-Hispanics were more likely to vote for Trump and younger voters and ethnic minorities were more likely to vote for Clinton. Those over the age of 45 favoured Trump, with a nine-point difference. In contrast, Clinton had a 12-point lead with the under-45 age group. There was a significant divide among the races, with almost 60% of white people supporting Trump and a staggering 88% of African Americans supporting Clinton.

(Total 2 marks: overall conclusion supported by detailed evidence from Source A and Source C)

Possible approaches to answering the question – the influence of gender and income on voting behaviour in the 2016 election:

Response 5

Women and low-income earners were more likely to vote for Clinton, and men and higher earners were more likely to vote for Trump.

(Total 0 marks: conclusion with no supporting evidence)

Response 6

Women and low-income earners were more likely to vote for Clinton, and men and higher earners were more likely to vote for Trump. Source B clearly shows a significant gender gap with a 13-pont lead for Clinton in female voting and an 11-point gap for Trump in male voting. Interestingly, married women were more likely to vote for Trump (Source A). In terms of income, Source B highlights the income difference. Those earning less than $40,000 voted in favour of Clinton by 12 points and those earning over $40,000 voted for Tump, but only by 2 points.

(Total marks 3: overall conclusion supported by detailed evidence)

Possible overall conclusion on the factor which most influenced the result of the USA presidential election:

Response 7

I conclude overall that the most important factor that influenced the result was Trump winning four out of the five key swing states.

(Total 1 mark: overall conclusion supported by evidence from Source A)

Response 8

I conclude overall that the most important factor that influenced the result was Trump winning four out of the five key swing states (Source A). Trump's combined lead in four of the swing states was only around 85,000 votes, yet he received 75 electoral votes and Clinton received none. In Michigan, for example, Trump won 47.3% of votes compared to Clinton's 47.0% and gained all of the 16 electoral votes (Source B).

(Total 2 marks: overall conclusion supported by detailed evidence)

Marks will not be awarded for a valid conclusion which is not supported with relevant source evidence.

---

2   You can be credited in a number of ways **up to a maximum of 10 marks.**

Evidence that supports the view (zero-hours contracts benefit only the employer):

▶ Source A, this benefits employers through lower wage bills and higher profits.
▶ Source A, many workers claim that these contracts prevent them from taking extra employment elsewhere even if they are only working for four hours a week.
▶ Source A, according to the TUC they can lead to poverty pay.
▶ Source C, there is a significant wage gap between those on non-zero-hours contracts, and those on zero-hours contracts – £510 gross weekly wage compared to £250.
▶ Source A, many young people feel trapped in these low-paid zero-hours contracts, which provide limited career progression.
▶ Source A, many workers feel exploited as they will not receive the benefits other workers are entitled to, such as redundancy payment.
▶ Source A, many workers on these contracts may be forced to use food banks and perhaps take out high-interest loans.
▶ Source B, 40% of those on a zero-hours contract would prefer more hours.
▶ Source C, zero-hours-contract employees work fewer hours.

Response 1

These contracts benefit only the employer as they do not need to provide redundancy pay and other benefits. This benefits employers through lower wage bills and higher profits. This is supported in Source C, which shows that there is a significant wage gap between those on non-zero-hours contracts and those on zero-hours contracts.

(Total 2 marks: evidence linked from two sources)

Evidence that opposes the view (zero-hours contracts benefit only the employer):

▶ Source A, the CBI states that these contracts have helped to create economic recovery and that unemployment is one of the lowest in Europe, so many workers have been able to find a job.
▶ Source A, young people have been able to find work; zero-hours contracts are highest among young people at 37%. Link to Source A, they provide flexibility for both employer and workers, especially students; link to Source B, greater work–life balance for those on zero-hours contracts – 65% to 58%.
▶ Source A, they provide crucial employment in rural areas.
▶ Source B, more workers are satisfied with zero-hours contracts – 60% to 59%. Link to Source A, many employees enjoy working on these contracts.
▶ Source A, these contracts can lead to a high turnover of staff, which can impact on the quality of work for the employer.

Response 2

These contracts can benefit the employee. Source A states that many employees enjoy these contracts, especially students and the retired.

(Total 1 mark: evidence used from one source)

For full marks, candidates must make an overall judgement as to the extent of the accuracy of the given statement.

Examples of possible overall judgements:

Response 3

The statement that zero-hours contracts benefit only the employer is accurate.

(Total 0 marks)

Response 4

The statement that zero-hours contracts benefit only the employer is not correct.

(Total 0 marks)

Response 5

Overall, it is largely accurate to state that zero-hours contracts benefit only the employer. These contracts provide far more benefits to the employer than to the employees – for example, employers do not need to give them a pension. Source C indicates that these workers are paid far less than other workers.

(Total 2 marks)

---

3 You can be credited in a number of ways **up to a maximum of 8 marks.**

Possible approaches to answering the question:

Source A

Response 1

Source A is reliable.

(Total 0 marks: no evidence or explanation provided)

Response 2

Source A is mostly reliable and trustworthy. It comes from a poll commissioned by the highly respected quality newspaper, *The Sunday Times*. The research also asked a large sample of over 1000 voters. This ensures that the information presented is representative.

(Total 2 marks: detailed evidence provided)

Source B

Response 3

Source B might be viewed as not being reliable as it was published almost ten years ago and might be out of date. However, it is factual information which is still relevant today.

(Total 1 mark: straightforward evidence provided)

Response 4

Source B might be viewed as not being reliable as it was published almost ten years ago and might be out of date. However, it is factual information which is still relevant today, and it was written for Higher Modern Studies students.

(Total 2 marks: detailed evidence provided)

Source C

Response 5

Source C can be viewed as not being reliable as it is produced by a pressure group trying to influence public opinion, and as such could be considered biased.

(Total 1 mark: straightforward evidence provided)

Response 6

Source C can be viewed as not being reliable as it is produced by a pressure group trying to influence public opinion, and as such could be considered biased. It is also possibly out of date as its evidence was produced in 2014.

(Total 2 marks: detailed evidence provided)

Examples of an overall conclusion on the most reliable source:

Response 7

Source A is the most reliable as it comes from a reputable source and contains a very high number of respondents to the survey.

(Total 1 mark: overall conclusion supported by evidence from one source)

Response 8

Source A is the most reliable as it comes from a reputable source and contains a very high number of respondents to the survey. The information is from 2019 and the survey takes place during the campaign to elect a new Conservative leader and Prime Minister. In contrast, the information in Source C is from a dated source and from a potentially biased organisation. Source B is dated and the information provided is very limited and complex.

(Total 2 marks: overall conclusion supported by detailed evidence from all sources)

For full marks, you must make an overall judgement on the most reliable source.

Paper 1

Section 1: Democracy in Scotland and the United Kingdom

1(a) You can be credited in a number of ways **up to a maximum of 20 marks.**

Credit responses that make reference to:

▶ possible alternatives for the governance of Scotland

▶ differences between the possible alternatives for the governance of Scotland

▶ comparison between the possible alternatives for the governance of Scotland.

Candidates may refer to:

▶ independence

▶ continuation of devolution

▶ federalism

▶ devo-max

▶ Westminster rule

▶ independence within Europe.

Possible approaches to answering the question:

Response 1

One possible alternative for Scotland's future is full independence. This is where Scotland has full control of all the powers within the country, such as tax-raising powers and responsibility for defence, and control of its own borders. In order to do this the Scottish people would have to vote for it through a referendum and break away from the rest of the UK.

(Total 1 mark: knowledge)

Response 2

One possible alternative for Scotland's future is full independence. This is where Scotland has full control of all the powers within the country, such as tax-raising powers and responsibility for defence, and control of its own borders. In order to do this the Scottish people would have to vote for it through a referendum and break away from the rest of the UK. The likelihood of this happening depends on whether Westminster would allow this. They allowed a vote on Scottish Independence in 2014, which the 'No' side won by 55% to 45%, but the Prime Minister has said that 'Now is not the time' in relation to a second vote. Also, the Scottish First Minister has said that she would demand a second referendum, 'When the time is right'. Therefore, while independence is an option, it seems a long way off.

(Total 3 marks: knowledge)

Response 3

One possible alternative for Scotland's future is full independence. This is where Scotland has full control of all the powers within the country, such as tax-raising powers and responsibility for defence, and control of its own borders. In order to do this the Scottish people would have to vote for it through a referendum and break away from the rest of the UK. The likelihood of this happening depends on whether Westminster would allow this. They allowed a vote on Scottish Independence in 2014, which the 'No' side won by 55% to 45%, but the Prime Minister has said that 'Now is not the time' in relation to a second vote. Also, the Scottish First Minister has said that she would demand a second referendum, 'When the time is right'. Therefore, while independence is an option, it seems a long way off, and in the meantime Scotland would be left with devolution, which means that Scotland has got some power over some areas to decide what happens in the country such as health, education and some limited powers over taxation. These are called devolved powers. However, it doesn't have complete control like independence. Some powers would still be decided by Westminster, such as defence and social security. Therefore, the difference between independence and devolution is that under independence Scotland would have full control, whereas with devolution, it only has full powers over some areas, but no power over others.

(Total 5 marks: 4 marks knowledge, 1 mark evaluation)

3(b) You can be credited in a number of ways **up to a maximum of 20 marks.**

Credit responses that make reference to:

▶ ways that Parliament can hold Government to account

▶ the extent to which Parliament can hold Government to account.

Candidates may refer to:

▶ type of government – e.g. majority, minority, coalition

▶ size of majority

▶ Prime Minister's Questions

▶ House of Lords

▶ debates and votes

▶ committees

▶ Private Members' Bills, Ten-Minute Rule Bills.

Possible approaches to answering the question:

Response 1

One way that Parliament can hold to account the work of Government is through Prime Minister's or Ministers' question time. This is where the Leader of the Opposition and backbench MPs get the opportunity to ask difficult questions of the Prime Minister and hold to account how they are running the country.

(Total 1 mark: knowledge)

Response 2

One way that Parliament can hold to account the work of Government is through Prime Minister's or Ministers' question time. This is where the Leader of the Opposition and backbench MPs get the opportunity to ask difficult questions of the Prime Minister and hold to account how they are running the country. Some people think that this is an effective way of holding the Government to account as it is televised live and the Prime Minister does not know what they are going to be asked. Therefore, there is potential for the Prime Minister to be embarrassed by a difficult question.

(Total 2 marks: 1 mark knowledge, 1 mark analysis)

Response 3

One way that Parliament can hold to account the work of Government is through Prime Minister's or Ministers' question time. This is where the Leader of the Opposition and backbench MPs get the opportunity to ask difficult questions of the Prime Minister and hold to account how they are running the country. Some people think that this is an effective way of holding the Government to account as it is televised live and the Prime Minister does not know what they are going to be asked. Therefore, there is potential for the Prime Minister to be embarrassed by a difficult question. However, some people think the Prime Minister's Questions are not a good way of holding the Government to account as often soft questions are asked of the PM by MPs from the same party and this can be used to waste some of the very limited time that there is for Prime Minister's Questions. Also, the Prime Minister is often well briefed on what kind of questions may be asked and can sidestep them or deflect from fully answering them. Another point is that it only occurs once a week for less than an hour, and this is often seen as not being enough time to adequately hold Government to account. Therefore, there is divided opinion on how effective this is at holding Government to account.

(Total 5 marks: 2 marks knowledge, 2 marks analysis, 1 mark evaluation)

3(c) You can be credited in a number of ways **up to a maximum of 20 marks.**

Credit responses that make reference to:

▶ strengths of voting systems

▶ weaknesses of voting systems

▶ comparison and comment on the extent of the strengths of some voting systems.

Candidates may refer to:

▶ First Past the Post

▶ Single Transferable Vote

▶ Additional Member system

- proportionality
- lack of proportionality
- choice
- representation
- voter–representative link.

Possible approaches to answering the question:

Response 1

One strength of voting systems can be the level of proportionality of the specific system – that is, how closely the percentage of votes received for a party matches the percentage of seats received. Some voting systems, such as the Single Transferable Vote system, are seen to be more proportional than a system such as First Past the Post.

(Total 1 mark: knowledge)

Response 2

One strength of voting systems can be the level of proportionality of the specific system – that is, how closely the percentage of votes received for a party matches the percentage of seats received. Some voting systems, such as the Single Transferable Vote (STV) system, are seen to be more proportional than a system such as First Past the Post (FPTP). This is seen as being a strength because it means that all voters have an equal say and are fairly represented under proportional systems such as STV, which is more democratic than FPTP, which tends to favour the larger, more established parties such as Labour and the Conservatives or the SNP in Scotland.

(Total 3 marks: 2 marks knowledge, 1 mark analysis)

Response 3

One strength of voting systems can be the level of proportionality of the specific system – that is, how closely the percentage of votes received for a party matches the percentage of seats received. Some voting systems, such as the Single Transferable Vote (STV) system, are seen to be more proportional than a system such as First Past the Post (FPTP). This is seen as being a strength because it means that all voters have an equal say and are fairly represented under proportional systems such as STV, which is more democratic than FPTP, which tends to favour the larger, more established parties such as Labour and the Conservatives or the SNP in Scotland. In the 2017 general election, which used FPTP, UKIP got almost 4 million votes but didn't get a single MP in Parliament. Whereas, the SNP got 1.4 million votes but won 56 seats. This is clearly not fair. Had STV been used then the result would have been much more proportional and fairer – for example UKIP would have won over 75 seats, which is a fairer representation of the number of votes cast for them. Therefore, one strength that STV has over FPTP is that it is fairer as it gives a much more proportional result and mirrors the percentage of votes cast more.

(Total 6 marks: 3 marks knowledge, 2 marks analysis, 1 mark evaluation)

Section 2: Social issues in the United Kingdom

2(a) You can be credited in a number of ways **up to a maximum of 12 marks.**

Credit responses that make reference to:

▶ examples of inequality on a specific group

▶ analysis of the impact of inequality on a specific group.

Candidates may refer to:

▶ types of inequality

▶ inequality within a group

▶ gender inequality

▶ poverty

▶ pensioner inequality

▶ race inequality

▶ child inequality

▶ access to education, jobs, promotion

▶ discrimination

▶ improvements or otherwise.

Possible approaches to answering the question:

Response 1

The type of inequality I have studied is gender inequality. Women are more likely than men to suffer inequality. Women are more likely to be working in poorer paid jobs and are more likely to receive, on average, poorer rates of pay than men.

(Total 1 mark: knowledge)

Response 2

The type of inequality I have studied is gender inequality. Women are more likely than men to suffer inequality. Women are more likely to be working in poorer paid jobs and are more likely to receive, on average, poorer rates of pay than men. Women are more likely to work in part-time jobs with little job security in areas known as the '5Cs' – catering, childcare, clerical, etc. The impact of this type of work is that their average earnings are over 15% less than men's and they are, therefore, more likely to suffer higher levels of poverty than men.

(Total 3 marks: 2 marks knowledge, 1 mark analysis)

Response 3

The type of inequality I have studied is gender inequality. Women are more likely than men to suffer inequality. Women are more likely to be working in poorer paid jobs and are more likely to receive, on average, poorer rates of pay than men. Women are more likely to work in part-time jobs with little job security in areas known as the '5Cs' – catering, childcare, clerical, etc. The impact of this type of work is that their average earnings are over 15% less than men's and they are, therefore, more likely to suffer higher levels of poverty than men. Women are also less likely to occupy promoted posts than men, despite women having higher levels of educational achievement in school and in further education. There are more Chief Executives called John in the top UK companies than there are women Chief Executives. That said, some women are breaking through the glass ceiling, particularly in areas such as law and medicine. This shows that there is some improvement in some employment areas, but not across every area.

(Total marks 5: 3 marks knowledge, 2 marks evaluation)

2(b) You can be credited in a number of ways **up to a maximum of 12 marks.**

Credit responses that make reference to:

▶ collectivist ideas in relation to inequality

▶ impact of collectivist ideas/policies in relation to inequality.

Candidates may refer to:

▶ collectivist ideas

▶ government responsibility

▶ individual responsibility

▶ examples of collectivist policies
▶ means testing
▶ differences between the UK's approach and Scotland's approach.

Possible approaches to answering the question:
Response 1
A collectivist is someone who believes that the Government should provide and meet the needs of those who most need it – for example, the sick, poor, unemployed and elderly. Political parties, such as the SNP or Corbyn's Labour, are collectivists. The Welfare State and the NHS are examples of collectivism.
(Total 2 marks: knowledge)

Response 2
A collectivist is someone who believes that the Government should provide and meet the needs of those who most need it – for example, the sick, poor, unemployed and elderly. Political parties, such as the SNP or Corbyn's Labour, are collectivists. The Welfare State and the NHS are examples of collectivism. Collectivists argue that inequalities are too wide to leave to the individual. Health and wealth inequalities are far too big to leave to the individual. This suggests that they would need the intervention of the Government to tackle this effectively, and to take control. This is evidence that only the Government can deliver the aims of the Welfare State, that it takes government action in order to create fairness and equality in society.
(Total 4 marks: 3 marks knowledge, 1 mark analysis)

Response 3
A collectivist is someone who believes that the Government should provide and meet the needs of those who most need it – for example, the sick, poor, unemployed and elderly. Political parties, such as the SNP or Corbyn's Labour, are collectivists. The Welfare State and the NHS are examples of collectivism. Collectivists argue that inequalities are too wide to leave to the individual. Health and wealth inequalities are far too big to leave to the individual. This suggests that they would need the intervention of the Government to tackle this effectively, and to take control. This is evidence that only the Government can deliver the aims of the Welfare State, that it takes government action in order to create fairness and equality in society. However, it is argued that we are individuals who should take responsibility for our own health and well-being. Many inequalities are created by people not taking responsibility for themselves. People make or take poor lifestyle choices that create inequality in society. The big three killers in Scotland are heart attacks, cancers and strokes, which can all be attributed to some degree to poor lifestyle choices. This shows that individuals must take responsibility for their own inequalities. Poor people tend to make poorer lifestyle choices, so in many ways they are victims of their own poor lifestyle choices.
(Total 6 marks: 4 marks knowledge, 2 marks analysis)

2(c) You can be credited in a number of ways **up to a maximum of 12 marks.**
Credit responses that make reference to:
▶ legal rights of UK citizens
▶ analysis of the impact and reasons for changes to legal rights of UK citizens.

Candidates may refer to:
▶ lack of UK written constitution enshrining UK rights
▶ changes to UK legal rights of citizens
▶ impact of Brexit on legal rights of UK citizens
▶ potential removal of Human Rights Act following Brexit
▶ new laws – for example, cyberterrorism, legal highs, OBFA (Offensive Behaviour at Football Act) repeal
▶ responses to terrorism laws.

Possible approaches to answering the question:
Response 1
The legal rights of UK citizens can change as, unlike the USA, we don't have a written constitution to protect the legal rights of UK citizens. All it takes is an Act of Parliament to remove some of the rights and freedoms that British citizens have.
(Total 1 Mark: knowledge)

Response 2

The legal rights of UK citizens can change as, unlike the USA, we don't have a written constitution to protect the legal rights of UK citizens. All it takes is an Act of Parliament to remove some of the rights and freedoms that British citizens have. The Conservatives are keen to remove the Human Rights Act should the UK ever leave the European Union. This would take away many of the UK citizens' rights. This shows that, while we are a free nation, many of the freedoms we take for granted could easily be removed if a government wished to do so and they had a large enough parliamentary majority.

(Total 3 marks: 2 marks knowledge, 1 mark analysis)

Response 3

The legal rights of UK citizens can change as, unlike the USA, we don't have a written constitution to protect the legal rights of UK citizens. All it takes is an Act of Parliament to remove some of the rights and freedoms that British citizens have. The Conservatives are keen to remove the Human Rights Act should the UK ever leave the European Union. This would take away many of the UK citizens' rights. This shows that, while we are a free nation, many of the freedoms we take for granted could easily be removed if a government wished to do so and they had a large enough parliamentary majority. New laws can be introduced, but laws can also be repealed and removed. For example, the Offensive Behaviour at Football Act was repealed following a Members' Bill by Labour MSP James Kelly, which managed to get enough MSPs from various parties to vote to remove it as it was unpopular.

(Total 4 marks: 3 marks knowledge, 1 mark analysis)

2(d) You can be credited in a number of ways **up to a maximum of 12 marks.**

Credit responses that make reference to:

▶ impact of crime on victims
▶ evaluation of impact of crime on victims.

Candidates may refer to:

▶ immediate physical impact
▶ psychological impact, increased fear
▶ emotional impact
▶ financial impact.

Possible approaches to answering the question:

Response 1

One impact of crime on victims is the immediate physical impact if they have been a victim of a crime where violence and aggression have been used. They may have physical injuries which may require hospital treatment and time to recover. Serious assaults and violence may prevent the victim from having a normal life while they recover from the crime.

(Total 1 mark: knowledge)

Response 2

One impact of crime on victims is the immediate physical impact if they have been a victim of a crime where violence and aggression have been used. They may have physical injuries which may require hospital treatment and time to recover. Serious assaults and violence may prevent the victim from having a normal life while they recover from the crime. This can also impact financially as they may not be able to work, and this can cost them in terms of lost pay while they are unable to work. They may even lose their job if they are unable to work for a long period of time and this could result in increased poverty for the victim. Therefore, we can see that one impact of crime can have consequences for the victim that impact on other areas such as an increased chance of poverty.

(Total 3 marks: 2 marks knowledge, 1 mark analysis)

Response 3

One impact of crime on victims is the immediate physical impact if they have been a victim of a crime where violence and aggression have been used. They may have physical injuries which may require hospital treatment and time to recover. Serious assaults and violence may prevent the victim from having a normal life while they recover from the crime. This can also impact financially as they may not be able to work and this can cost them in terms of lost pay while they are unable to work. They may even lose their job if they are unable to work for a long period of time and this could result in increased poverty for the victim. Therefore, we can see that one impact of crime can have consequences for the victim that impact on other areas such as an increased chance of poverty. In terms of who are likely to be victims of crime, young males are more likely to be victims. The elderly are also very vulnerable and it can lead to their isolation as they might be afraid to go out.

(Total 4 marks: 2 marks knowledge, 2 marks analysis)

Section 3: International issues

3(a) You can be credited in a number of ways **up to a maximum of 20 marks.**

Credit responses that make reference to:
- ▶ nature of social inequality
- ▶ extent of social inequality.

Candidates may refer to:
- ▶ healthcare
- ▶ housing
- ▶ education
- ▶ criminal justice.

Possible approaches to answering the question – world power: the USA:

Response 1

One way that social inequality can impact on African Americans is through access to healthcare. Many African Americans struggle to have adequate access to healthcare due to being uninsured or not being able to afford to pay for ongoing health treatment.

(Total 1 mark: knowledge)

Response 2

One way that social inequality can impact on African Americans is through access to healthcare. Many African Americans struggle to have adequate access to healthcare due to being uninsured or not being able to afford to pay for ongoing health treatment. This impacts on their overall health and can lead to them having lower life expectancy and higher incidences of morbidity than other American citizens. This shows that African Americans suffer social inequality with regard to healthcare.

(Total 2 marks: knowledge)

Response 3

One way that social inequality can impact on African Americans is through access to healthcare. Many African Americans struggle to have adequate access to healthcare due to being uninsured or not being able to afford to pay for ongoing health treatment. This impacts on their overall health and can lead to them having lower life expectancy and higher incidences of morbidity than other American citizens. This shows that African Americans suffer social inequality with regard to healthcare. To overcome this, President Obama introduced what was known as 'Obamacare' to guarantee a minimum level and access to healthcare for the 49 million Americans, many of them African American, who were uninsured or had no access to healthcare. This may now be under threat as President Trump has pledged to try to remove Obamacare. This shows that while progress has been made, there is a danger that social inequality with regard to healthcare could get worse.

(Total 4 marks: 3 marks knowledge, 1 mark analysis)

3(b) You can be credited in a number of ways **up to a maximum of 20 marks.**

Credit responses that make reference to:
- ▶ opportunities for participation
- ▶ limits to participation.

Candidates may refer to:
- ▶ ways of participating – interest groups, voting, unions, standing as a candidate
- ▶ under-representation, poor turnout, cost prohibitive.

Possible approaches to answering the question – world power: the USA:

Response 1

In the USA there are many opportunities for participation in the political process. People can join a political party and put themselves forward as a candidate for a post such as Senator or Mayor.

(Total 1 mark: knowledge)

Response 2

In the USA, there are many opportunities for participation in the political process. People can join a political party and put themselves forward as a candidate for a post such as Senator or Mayor. They have certain political rights guaranteed under the Constitution which means that they are a very democratic nation with lots of opportunities for people to get active in the political process.

(Total 3 marks: 2 marks knowledge, 1 mark analysis)

Response 3

In the USA, there are many opportunities for participation in the political process. People can join a political party and put themselves forward as a candidate for a post such as Senator or Mayor. They have certain political rights guaranteed under the Constitution which means that they are a very democratic nation with lots of opportunities for people to get active in the political process. However, putting yourself forward for election and running a campaign can be very expensive, which means that it is mostly wealthy Americans who can afford to stand or run as a candidate. This demonstrates that while there are plenty of opportunities to participate, many Americans are excluded from participation due to the cost.

(Total 5 marks: 3 marks knowledge, 2 marks analysis)

3(c) You can be credited in a number of ways **up to a maximum of 20 marks.**

Credit responses that make reference to:

▶ causes of the issue

▶ reasons why these causes have led to the issue.

Candidates may refer to:

▶ social causes

▶ economic causes

▶ political causes

▶ importance of the causes in creating the issue.

Possible approaches to answering the question – world issue: terrorism:

Response 1

One political cause of terrorism is lack of democracy in a country. This means that some people may feel that they don't have an opportunity for their voice to be heard in a dictatorship with little or no political rights and may resort to terrorism.

(Total 1 mark: knowledge)

Response 2

One political cause of terrorism is lack of democracy in a country. This means that some people may feel that they don't have an opportunity for their voice to be heard in a dictatorship with little or no political rights and may resort to terrorism. In Turkey, the Kurdish people feel as if the Government disregard their concerns and desire for self-governance. This has led to them using terrorist acts to try to get the Government to listen and act on their demands.

(Total 2 marks: knowledge)

Response 3

One political cause of terrorism is lack of democracy in a country. This means that some people may feel that they don't have an opportunity for their voice to be heard in a dictatorship with little or no political rights and may resort to terrorism. In Turkey, the Kurdish people feel as if the Government disregard their concerns and desire for self-governance. This has led to them using terrorist acts to try to get the Government to listen and act on their demands, which has resulted in them bombing targets such as the police, politicians and the army. This shows that there are political causes to terrorism, particularly if a group feels that the Government are ignoring them and not allowing them a say in how their region or country is run.

(Total 3 marks: 2 marks knowledge, 1 mark analysis)

3(d) You can be credited in a number of ways **up to a maximum of 20 marks.**

Credit responses that make reference to:

▶ impact of issue on wider international community

▶ extent of issue on wider international community.

Candidates may refer to:

▶ social impact

▶ economic impact

▶ political impact.

Possible approaches to answering this question – world issue: terrorism:

Response 1

One impact of terrorism on the international community is that it can cost them financially in trying to tackle the issue in terms of increased security and intelligence costs.

(Total 1 mark: knowledge)

Response 2

One impact of terrorism on the international community is that it can cost them financially in trying to tackle the issue in terms of increased security and intelligence costs. It can also have a social impact that can end up being financially costly. For example, increased terrorism in Syria has led to an influx of refugees into Europe, which has led to increased costs for those countries receiving refugees.

(Total 2 marks: knowledge)

Response 3

One impact of terrorism on the international community is that it can cost them financially in trying to tackle the issue in terms of increased security and intelligence costs. It can also have a social impact that can end up being financially costly. For example, increased terrorism in Syria has led to an influx of refugees into Europe which has led to increased costs for those countries receiving refugees. For example, Germany has received around 1 million refugees from Syria, which has proved very costly in terms of re-housing, educating and resettling them. This has also led to some social tensions in Germany between some of the refugees and German citizens who object to them. This shows that there is an impact across social and economic issues due to terrorism.

(Total 4 marks: 3 marks knowledge, 1 mark analysis)

Paper 2

1   You can be credited in a number of ways **up to a maximum of 10 marks.**

Possible approaches to answering the question – the fairness of the FPTP electoral system:

Response 1

The FPTP system is unfair as there can be a significant difference between the parties in terms of votes received and seats achieved. This is supported in Source A which highlights, according to the Electoral Reform Society, the failure of FPTP 'to accurately reflect the wishes of the British electorate' with, for example, Labour increasing its votes yet ending up with fewer seats – 26 fewer. Also, UKIP gained about 4 million votes (almost 10% of the votes) but received only one seat. FPTP distorts the voting wishes of the electorate.

(Total 3 marks: synthesis between Sources A, B and C and conclusion)

Response 2

The FPTP electoral system, while unfair throughout the UK, had its worst overall effects in Scotland. Thanks to FPTP the 'tartan tsunami' swept away Labour dominance, with Labour losing 40 of its 41 seats. Such is the unfairness of FPTP that the Scottish unionist parties won only three seats between them (5% of the seats) yet received over 46% of the votes.

(Total 2 marks: synthesis of evidence across Sources A and B with conclusion)

Response 3

Opinion polls failed to predict the outcome of the election and failed to understand the impact of FPTP.

(Total 0 marks: inaccurate conclusion)

Possible approaches to answering the question – the performance of the UK political parties in England and Wales compared to Scotland:

Response 4

There are clear differences between the performance of political parties in England and Wales and Scotland. Conservatives were strong in England and Wales, winning 330 of the 574 seats, while the SNP won 56 of the 59 Scottish seats.

(Total 1 mark: conclusion and correct use of Source B)

Response 5

There are clear differences between the performance of political parties in England and Wales and Scotland. Conservatives were strong in England and Wales, winning 330 of the 574 seats, while the SNP won 56 of the 59 Scottish seats. Also, minority parties such as UKIP performed well in terms of votes in England, but not in Scotland. In England, UKIP won over 14.1% of the votes, but less than 2% in Scotland. Labour increased its number of seats in England by 15 but suffered a disaster in Scotland, losing 40 of its 41 seats.

(Total 2 marks: synthesis of evidence across Sources A and B with conclusion)

Possible approaches to answering the question – the accuracy of opinion polls compared to the actual result:

Response 6

One conclusion is that opinion polls failed to reflect the actual national election result. Source A states that it was predicted that the election would be very close, but no party would win an overall majority. However, Source C shows that while it was fairly close, the Conservatives did win an overall majority. Thus showing that the opinion polls failed to reflect the national result.

(Total 2 marks: conclusion with evidence)

Response 7

One conclusion that could be drawn about the accuracy of opinion polls is that they were more accurate about the Scottish result than they were for the overall UK result. Source A states that opinion polls failed 'to reflect the actual national election result' but 'were far more accurate when it came to Scotland'. Source C shows that the opinion polls were wrong for the UK, where there was an overall winner, but got it correct in Scotland as there was a clear winner, with the SNP winning 50 of the 56 seats which was in line with the 'clear winner' opinion poll prediction.

(Total 3 marks: conclusion with detailed evidence)

Possible overall conclusion on the results of the 2015 general election:

Response 8

Overall, the evidence from each of the Sources A–C does suggest that FPTP creates a wide gap between the votes a party receives and the number of seats it actually wins.

(Total 0 marks: overall conclusion without supporting evidence)

Response 9

One overall conclusion is that opinion polls failed to reflect the actual national result. Opinion polls had suggested that no party would win an overall majority. However, the Conservatives gained 25 seats, which gave them 331 seats and an overall majority.

(Total 2 marks: valid overall conclusion based on evidence from two sources)

Marks will not be awarded for a valid conclusion which is not supported with relevant source evidence.

2   You can be credited in a number of ways **up to a maximum of 10 marks.**

Evidence that supports the view (an outstanding victory for the ANC):
▶ Source A, the ANC has won five elections in a row and won 11 million of the 18 million votes cast.
▶ Source A, the ANC won over 60% of the vote and eight of the nine provinces.
▶ Source A, gained more than 70% in three of the provinces.
▶ Source B, won 62.1% of votes.
▶ Source B, the ANC have 249 MPs compared to nearest rivals the DA, who have only 89 MPs.
▶ Source C, the ANC gained almost 80% of votes in Limpopo.

Response 1

It was an outstanding victory for the ANC as they won 11 million of the 18 million votes, and this is further supported by the fact that the ANC dominate Parliament, with 249 MPs compared to only 89 for the DA.

(Total 2 marks: evidence linked from two sources)

Evidence that opposes the view (an outstanding victory for the ANC):
▶ Source A, the ANC received its lowest ever support.
▶ Source A, the ANC failed to win back the Western Cape, which it had lost in 2009.
▶ Source A, the DA gained an extra 1 million votes.
▶ Source A, many South Africans are disillusioned with the ANC.
▶ Source B, the ANC vote declined by 4% and they lost 15 seats.
▶ Source C, the ANC only won 33% of the votes in Western Cape and its vote declined in Gauteng by 10%.

Response 2

It was not an outstanding victory as the ANC did not regain the Western Cape and only received about a third of the votes in that province.

(Total 2 marks: evidence linked from two sources)

For full marks, you must make an overall judgement as to the extent of the accuracy of the given statement.

Examples of possible overall judgements:

Response 3

The statement is partly correct: the ANC dominates Parliament and only lost one province.

(Total 1 mark)

Response 4

The statement is true to a certain extent.

(Total 0 marks)

Response 5

The statement is only partially true. It could be argued (Source A) that it was outstanding for the ANC to win five elections in a row with 11 million of the 18 million votes cast, and in Source B to win 249 seats in the national Parliament. However, Source A indicates that the ANC had a disappointing result in Gauteng and failed to win back the Western Cape, gaining only 32.8% of the votes there (Source C). Therefore, it was not 'an outstanding victory for the ANC across the country'.

(Total 2 marks)

3 You can be credited in a number of ways **up to a maximum of 8 marks.**

Source A

Response 1

Source A is reliable.

(Total 0 marks: no evidence or explanation provided)

Response 2

Source A is reliable as it is election results from the 2017 UK general election, which is fairly up to date.

(Total 1 mark: straightforward evidence provided)

Response 3

Source A is reliable and trustworthy. The statistics presented are actual results from the 2017 UK general election. These are facts and cannot be manipulated to alter or change the result. The results are from all of the 650 constituencies and have been collected under UK election law, which makes them highly trustworthy.

(Total 2 marks: detailed evidence provided)

Source B

Response 4

Source B can be seen to be not that reliable as it comes from the Facebook page of a Liberal Democrat supporter whose comments are one-sided and could be accused of using exaggeration. Words such as 'stunning' and 'humiliated' display obvious bias, therefore making it less reliable However, the figures quoted are from the August 2019 Welsh by-election, which makes it up to date with relevant political information.

(Total 2 marks: detailed evidence provided)

Source C

Response 5

Source C can be seen to be very reliable as it comes from a highly reputable polling organisation, Ipsos MORI. It also uses a large sample size of around 1000 voters, which makes it more reliable than a smaller sample size. The respondents are all of voting age of 18+, but it doesn't state if they were a representative sample of the entire UK population, which may make it not fully representative and therefore not as reliable as first thought.

(Total 2 marks: detailed evidence provided)

Example of an overall conclusion on the most reliable source:

Response 6

Source A is the most reliable source as the information presented is factual and based upon election results carried out under UK election law. Source C can also be seen to be reliable as it was carried out by a highly reputable company, but it didn't state how representative the respondents were of the entire UK population. Source B is probably the least reliable as it comes from the social media page of a Liberal Democrat supporter and is more likely to be one-sided and not fully balanced. Overall, sources A and C are more reliable than source B, with the most reliable being source A as it is factual information.

(Total 2 marks: overall conclusion supported by detailed evidence from all sources)

For full marks, you must make an overall judgement on the most reliable source.

Revision notes

Revision notes

Have you seen our full range of revision and exam practice resources?

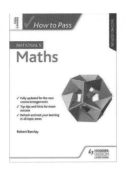